John Jay, Bayard Tuckerman

William Jay and the Constitutional Movement for the Abolition of Slavery

John Jay, Bayard Tuckerman

William Jay and the Constitutional Movement for the Abolition of Slavery

ISBN/EAN: 9783744709590

Printed in Europe, USA, Canada, Australia, Japan

Cover: Foto ©ninafisch / pixelio.de

More available books at **www.hansebooks.com**

WILLIAM JAY

AND

THE CONSTITUTIONAL MOVEMENT FOR
THE ABOLITION OF SLAVERY

BY
BAYARD TUCKERMAN

WITH A PREFACE BY
JOHN JAY

NEW-YORK
DODD, MEAD & COMPANY
1894

PREFACE

BY JOHN JAY.

A PROLONGED illness, added to other causes, has disappointed my hope of completing an elaborate biography of my father.

This memoir by Mr. Tuckerman is devoted chiefly to the part borne by Judge Jay in the antislavery work, to which his time and thoughts were so long given. In this connection the memoir develops his personal characteristics, with the constitutional principles and national policy advocated by him in that historic contest; while of necessity it touches but lightly on his home life, his varied correspondence, and his judicial charges, one of which assisted to avert the passage of a pro-slavery legislative act infringing the liberty of speech and of the press; and the scope of the volume forbids its dwelling on his writings on other topics, some of which are still subjects of discussion.

Judge Jay's memoir on the formation of a National Bible Society, which in 1816 so warmly encouraged the hopes of the venerable Boudinot, was followed by spirited controversial pamphlets with an antagonist as able and eminent as Bishop Hobart. The correspondence after Jay's first letter was marked by an unusual sharpness, which happily did not prevent my cherished and lamented friend, the son and namesake of the Bishop, from becoming in later years sincerely attached to his father's antagonist. It was a contest in which Jay vindicated the right of Churchmen to assist in the distribution of the Bible, and anticipated in this his similar efforts for a lifetime to secure the united action of all good citizens, without regard to creed or politics, in practicable schemes for the elevation and happiness of mankind. Among his earlier essays were two on "Sunday: Its Value as a Civil Institution, and Its Sacred Character"; while a third, upon "Duelling as a Relic of Barbarism," was honoured, when the authorship was still unknown, by a medal from an anti-duelling association at Savannah.

THE LIFE OF JOHN JAY.

Judge Jay, in the life of his father, which was welcomed as an important addition to our American biography of the Revolution, vindicated, by a careful presentation of the historical evidence then available, the soundness of the judgment of Jay and Adams, as peace commissioners at Paris in 1782-83, regarding the policy of the French court as unfriendly to the American claims to the boundaries, the fisheries, and the Mississippi. That judgment, afterwards acquiesced in by Dr. Franklin in the joint violation by the commissioners of the instructions of Congress—a violation that enabled them to obtain from England boundaries and concessions far greater than either Congress or France expected—had been roughly criticised and denied, even in volumes of diplomatic correspondence claiming an official sanction. Its vindication by Judge Jay has recently been more than confirmed by the ample proofs published by M. de Circourt in the secret correspondence of the Count de Vergennes with his able corps of diplomatic agents, as well as by the interesting revelations in Lord Edmond Fitzmaurice's "Life of Lord Shelburne"; and these volumes have dissipated a cloud of error which for half a century travestied the facts and dimmed the glory of the closing act of the American Revolution.*

JAY'S "WAR AND PEACE," AND INTERNATIONAL ARBITRATION.

Judge Jay's little book on "War and Peace," with a plan of stipulation by treaty for international arbitration which subsequently led to his becoming the president of the American Peace Society, and which before its publication attracted the attention of that sturdy advocate for peace, Joseph Sturge, during his visit at Bedford, seems entitled to special notice as one whose scheme is still agitated in the governmental and national councils of Europe. The plan promptly received the approval of the Peace Society of London,

---

* The title of M. de Circourt's work is:—"*Histoire de l'action commune de la France et de l'Amerique pour l'Indépendence des États Unis.*" Paris, 1876.

and of English statesmen like Richard Cobden and the indefatigable Henry Richard. It exercised a European influence in the highest quarters when its spirit, under the leadership of Lord Clarendon, received the sanction of the great powers of Europe who signed the Treaty at Paris in 1856. Its endorsement, while cautiously expressed, was recognized as having a new and profound significance. The Protocol No. 23 declared the wish of the signatory governments that states between which any serious misunderstanding might arise should, before appealing to arms, have recourse, as far as circumstances might allow, to the good offices of a friendly power; it being understood that the wish expressed by Congress should not in any case oppose limits to that liberty of appreciation which no power could alienate in questions that touched its dignity. With that limitation the recommendation, in advance of a resort to war to have recourse to a friendly power, was introduced by the Congress to the International Code of Europe; and among those great diplomatists were the Count Walewski and Baron Bourgueny, on the part of France; Count de Buol-Shauenstein and Baron de Hubner, on the part of Austria; Lord Clarendon and Lord Cowley, on the part of Great Britain; Count Orloff and Baron de Bruno, on the part of Russia; and Count Cavour and the Marquis de Villamarina, on the part of Sardinia. The action of the Congress was subsequently confirmed by that of the lesser states of Europe. Mr. Gladstone pronounced the protocol " a very great triumph, a powerful engine in behalf of civilized humanity." The late Earl of Derby referred to it as "the principle which to its immortal honour was embodied in the protocols of the Conference at Paris"; and the Earl of Malmesbury pronounced the act "one important to civilization and to the security of the peace of Europe." The idea that this scheme is more and more regarded as widely applicable to international disputes, as easily practicable and profoundly important to the peace of nations, would seem probable from the extent to which, as the century approaches its completion, the scheme has occupied more and more the attention of both the statesmen and of the masses who are the most interested in discovering a substitute for war.

For a time after the Geneva award, the moral weight and value of international arbitration seemed to be more doubted than ever. It was said that while the scheme had in that case avoided war, it had suggested the probability of claims so extravagant and inadmissible as almost to force the opposing party to break the treaty under the cover of which they were advanced, even at the risk of increased hostility and a resort to war; and that the escape of both nations from such a catastrophe by the action of the Genevan Court in dismissing without argument the American claims for indirect damages was but a happy accident. But this idea seems to have been succeeded by the happier thought that an appeal to international arbitration is an appeal to the fairness of the world, and that the question for the parties, judges, and spectators is so clearly one of honour, that no nation can afford to ask what the justice of the world candidly disapproves. In the case of the Geneva Congress, while the rejected claims were presented in the name of the President, General Grant himself subsequently denied their justice and approved their rejection. Sir Lyon (now Lord) Playfair, who perhaps appreciates the entire subject of arbitration as thoroughly as any living statesman, gave an interesting sketch of its recent progress, both in Europe and America, in a paper entitled, "A Topic for Christmas," in the *North American Review* for December, 1890. Three years before, Sir Lyon had headed a deputation of members of the English Parliament who came to present to the President of the United States a memorial from 234 members of the House of Commons, with delegates from English Trades Unions representing 700,000 workingmen. Congress in response concurrently resolved to invite from time to time, as fit occasion might arise, negotiations with any government with which the United States has or may have diplomatic relations, to the end that any differences or disputes arising between the two governments which cannot be settled by diplomatic agency may be referred to arbitration and be peacefully adjusted by such means. Although Europe is supposed by many to be awaiting a war of gigantic magnitude, Sir Lyon, referring to the approval of arbitration by the Pan-American Congress by continental parliaments and international assemblies at Paris and London, said that the legislatures which had already passed resolutions in favor of arbitration represented 150,000,000 of people, and remarked that the extension of that feeling would be a better force than an international police to secure the observance of treaties. The excess of war preparation already endangering national credit and threatening national bankruptcy is quoted as proving that the arbitration idea will be insisted upon, and in the anticipated movement the United States is described as fitted to be the leading champion of arbitration. Sheridan is quoted among others as saying: "I mean what I say when I express the belief that arbitration will rule the world." The scheme is now represented as likely to be accepted by thinkers who reject the thought of Kant, Bentham, and Mills for an international Congress; and Sir Lyon Playfair, in connection with the idea of arbitration, quotes the remark of Mazzini that "thought is the action of men and action the thought of the people."

"THE WAR WITH MEXICO," AND ANTISLAVERY PAPERS.

The "Review of the War with Mexico" stands among Judge Jay's volumes unexcelled by exactness of congressional, diplomatic, and, to some extent, military research; and by plainness of speech in regard to national outrages and perfidy without a name, perpetrated in the cause of slavery; and his writings generally on this subject show the same accurate inquiry and outspoken frankness. It was on the varied phases of our treatment of the coloured people, free and slave, at our own doors, the cruel wrong so full of injustice to the blacks, of scandal to Christendom, and of menace to the republic, that Jay wrote with deepest earnestness, the most exacting research, and a fearless pen. His inquiry into "The American Colonization and the Antislavery Societies" and "The Action of the Federal Government in Behalf of Slavery," developed facts which implicated prominent politicians of both parties, and aroused at once their surprise and indignation, while the disclosure directly appealed to the pride and conscience of the American people. The same judicial, dauntless, and defiant spirit marked the appeals which he prepared for the Antislavery Society against the calumnies of the press, and the dignified protest against the libellous charges so unworthily made by President Jackson in his message to Congress. The same spirit animated his address on "The Condition of the People of Colour in the United States"; the "Appeal to the Friends of Constitutional Liberty, on the Violation by the House of Representatives of the Right of Petition"; his supplement to "The Reproof of the American Church," by Bishop Wilberforce of Oxford; the exposure in the letter to Bishop Ives of the clerical efforts to sanctify slavery and caste; and his earnest demand for the equal admission of the coloured churches to the Diocesan Council of New York. So, too, with the critical analysis of Mr. Clay's "Compromise Bill," including the Fugitive Law and Mr.

Webster's "Theory of Physical Geography"; his address to the inhabitants of New Mexico and California, so timely distributed in English and Spanish, and so happily followed in California by a free constitution, urging them to resist the domination of slavery with its ignorance and degradation, and to secure, by their own manly independence and just statesmanship, a glorious future of power and happiness; his address to the antislavery Christians; and his plain reminders to the Protestant Episcopal Church, and to the Tract and other societies, of the inconsistency and evil influence of their compromising pro-slavery policy.

CONSTITUTIONAL PRINCIPLES—AN HISTORIC PARALLEL.

The part of Jay's life pictured by Mr. Tuckerman not only exhibits these characteristics, but shows the Antislavery Society to have been founded by his care, in 1833, on constitutional principles so just and so clearly defined, that in 1839 sixteen hundred and fifty auxiliary societies had been established on the same basis, educating the rising generation, on whom was to rest the destiny of the country in the near future. It was an education of the quiet and effective influence of which the pro-slavery leaders seemed unconscious, although to some it may recall the thought of Dr. Storrs, when he said:—" When I think of a millennium in our time, in our civilization, my thought rests and fastens on the promise, 'a little child shall lead them.'" The charge had already been made against the opponents of slavery of a disregard of constitutional obligations—of a desire to dissolve the Union and to encourage slave insurrection. The society declared the exclusive right of each slave State to legislate in regard to slavery; the constitutional right of Congress to abolish slavery in the District of Columbia, to prohibit it in the Territories and new States, and to control the domestic as well as the foreign slave trade; and it disclaimed the idea of countenancing the slaves in vindicating their rights by resorting to physical force. And here is suggested, by the action and the anticipation of the Slave Power, an interesting historic parallel. The formation of the Antislavery Society in December, 1833, followed closely upon Mr. Calhoun's Nullification in South Carolina in 1832, when, as Mr. Pollard tell us, a medal was struck inscribed, "John C. Calhoun, First President of the C. S. A." A counterpart of this medal in gold is said to exist at Richmond, with the name of Jefferson Davis as the first president of the Southern Confederacy, and "1861" on the reverse side.

These incidents seem to emphasize the fact that the constitutional principles adopted by the Antislavery Society in 1833, and so widely circulated by the press and its auxiliaries before the war, although often assailed, were, in 1854, made the basis of the Republican party, which, as Americans of all sections may now with mutual regard and affection thank God, maintained the Union and abolished slavery. Such a revolution in public opinion is a forcible reminder of the truth that every principle contains within itself the germ of a prophecy, and it is a thought fraught with hope and confidence to reformers even when they seem to be threatened with disaster and defeat.

THE EARLY SCHEME FOR A SOUTHERN CONFEDERACY.

The determination to found a confederacy with slavery as its cornerstone appears as a fundamental feature in the policy of the Slave Power for some thirty years before the outbreak of the Civil War. Mr. Calhoun's idea of secession, apparently suggested by the tariff, General Jackson predicted would be renewed on the question of slavery. The novel of Prof. Beverly Tucker in 1835, entitled, "The Partisan Leader; or, Twenty Years After," foreshadowed the steps at home and abroad which were taken in forming the new confederacy; and in the South Carolina Convention in 1860, Southern politicians like Rhett, Parker, Keith, and Inglis said that the matter had nothing to do with Mr. Lincoln or the Fugitive Law, but had been culminating for a long series of years. The thought of a Southern Confederacy may have stimulated the policy of using the power of the Republic, while it lasted, in the interest of the Confederacy that was to succeed it; supplying a motive for the Texan Rebellion, the War with Mexico, the effort to secure Cuba, the filibustering expeditions to Central America, the determination to reopen the African slave-trade, and the pro-slavery action of the Buchanan administration.

NORTHERN AND EUROPEAN SYMPATHY WITH SLAVERY.

It would be hardly fair to the Southern leaders to assume that they found no reason for their hope of effecting the dissolution of the Union in the sympathy and aid promised from the North and from Europe. The secret conferences with Lord Lyons of Northern sympathizers with slavery were disclosed by the despatches of that eminent diplomatist. Mayor Fernando Wood's proposition that New York should become a free city, independent both of the States and the nation, showed in no slight degree the temper of the citizens whom he represented; while the later appeal of so eminent and popular a leader as Governor Horatio Seymour to the citizens of the State was equally significant when he said, "In the downfall of the nation, and amid its crumbling ruins, we will cling to the fortunes of New York." Such utterances enforced by leaders of the prominence of Franklin Pierce and Vallandingham; the political action of sympathizers with slavery and the anti-draft riots in New York, supplemented by the unfriendliness of European governments; and the escape of the "Alabama"—all these circumstances tended to encourage the hopes that were doomed to disappointment. Nor in considering the antislavery movement should we overlook the effect of the antislavery opinion of our country in ending the danger of European intervention, which had been unwittingly encouraged by Mr. Seward's too hasty assurance to our minister in France (April 22, 1861), that "the revolution was without a cause, without a pretext, and without an object; and that the condition of slavery in the several States would remain just the same, whether it should succeed or fail." The antislavery policy, first of enlistment and then of emancipation, so earnestly urged upon Mr. Lincoln and adopted by him with conscientious caution, enlightened Europe as to the true meaning of the contest in our recognition of the equal right to freedom and the equal dignity of labour, and forbade its rulers to assist in the establishment of a slave confederacy; and the historian Lessing, when alluding to the cordial reception by his holiness the Sovereign Pontiff of the diplomatic agents of Mr. Jefferson Davis, and the Papal letter recognizing and commending "the illustrious President of the Southern Confederacy," remarks that this was " the only official recognition of the chief conspirator by the head of any government." Nor should the right appreciation by the abolitionists of the prospect of freedom for the slaves be forgotten. The fidelity of the negroes during the war, both to the families with whom they lived, to which Vice-President Stephens bore distinct testimony, and to the Northern army, from which they expected emancipation, was no less honourable and conspicuous than the devotion and gallantry they constantly exhibited in the war, as at Fort Hudson and Fort Wagner, at Milliken's Bend and Lake Providence, at Newbern and at Olustee, where their rear-guard saved the army. Their conduct, whether at home or in the field, justified the conviction of their steadfast friends in the safety of immediate emancipation, and added untold force to the sacredness of the pledges so often given during the war, and still, to the national discredit, unfulfilled—of national aid to State education, so as to secure to every child of our coloured citizens the ability to read his Bible and the Constitution, to fulfill his duties and protect his rights.

As time and reflection impress upon the American mind a clear comprehension of the changes, national, social, and political, that a triumph of the Slave Power would have brought to America and its effect as a set-back to the civilization of the world, an increased interest will be felt in the beginnings of the contest, and in the men and causes that shaped its end.

THE LESSON FOR TO-DAY.

I cordially recommend Mr. Tuckerman's memoir to the students of the antislavery contest, as throwing light on that interesting and but partially written chapter of American history, in which my father bore a part; and on the character and policy of the sturdy band with whom he was associated, including Arthur and Lewis Tappan, Joshua Leavitt, James G. Birney, Gerrit Smith, and their true-hearted compatriots; while a wider view would include a group of noble women, who, if differing as to means, were united in devotion, headed by the honoured names of Maria Weston Chapman and Harriet Beecher

Stowe, Lucretia Mott, Lydia Maria Child, and the sisters Grimké.

Among our citizens who will be long remembered as early and fearless opponents of slavery, leading and acting with energy and independence, according to their personal convictions and occasionally in differing ways, were the venerable Isaac T. Hopper, William Lloyd Garrison, whose life has been so faithfully recorded by his sons, John Greenleaf Whittier, whose old Huguenot spirit lives in his verse as in his name, Ellis Gray Loring, Lovejoy, the martyr of the west, Wendell Phillips, with his matchless eloquence, Theodore D. Weld, with his trenchant pen, Elizur Wright, Jr., Samuel R. Ward, William Goodell, S. S. Jocelyn, Gamaliel Bailey, Jr., Edmund Quincey, S. H. Gay, Oliver Johnston, James S. Gibbons, and others, who opened the way—sometimes by devious and diverging paths—for the party of the Union and Emancipation.

As the contest advanced from the field of politics to that of war, came Union men from different points whose names will live in our history with those of John A. Andrew, John C. Fremont, John P. Hale, Chase, Sumner, Seward, Preston and John A. King, Wilmot, Giddings, Wade, Holt, and Edwin D. Stanton. In New York, where mob law had prevailed, the Union League Club upheld the loyalty of the city, the credit of the nation, and the sanitary commission; raised troops for Hancock in addition to its own coloured regiments; stimulated the ardour of our soldiers and the patriotism of the country; welcomed, of the army, Grant and Sherman, Mead and Sheridan, Hancock and Hooker, Warren and Burnside, and of the navy, Farragut, Dupont and Rogers, Winslow and the youthful Cushing; verifying in its spirit and action the remark of Vice-President Colfax that on the Union League Club Lincoln had leaned in the darkest hours.

The Club did not forget, neither will the truthful historian forget, that amid the European plots and intrigues in the interest of slavery, we had friends high and low, from Alexander of Russia, the emancipator of twenty millions of serfs—who, like Lincoln, fell by assassination—to the humble peasants, who instinctively recognised the hostility to the rights of labor inherent in the slavery system, whose vicious features had been exposed by John Bright with such masterly effect.

Goldwin Smith, the historic scholar of Oxford, who at home had denounced those who would have made England an accomplice in "the creation of a great slave empire, and in its future extension from the grave of Washington to the Halls of Montezuma," in his reply to the greetings of the eminent citizens who had asked him to the club and who assembled to meet him,[*] said, "Your cause is ours; it is the cause of the whole human race." The same idea, in almost the same words, was expressed by the Count de Cavour

---

[*] In view of their historic significance, their names are given in the Appendix.

a few days before his death, in a despatch to the Italian Minister at Washington, when he said "that ours was the cause not only of constitutional liberty, but of all humanity."

The antislavery story from the Calhoun medal, struck to commemorate the supposed birth of a slave empire to the constitutional abolition of slavery, concerned humanity, and has lessons of warning and encouragement for the men and women of to-day, on whom rest the hopes of the country, and who, against odds that seem as formidable as those presented by the Slave Power at its culmination, are bravely striving for the advance of humanity, the purification of our politics, and the preservation of American institutions. They may well adopt the inspiriting legend of Geneva to which the antislavery contest of America has given a new radiance, "Post tenebras lux." Our institutions, no longer endangered by slavery, are assailed with skilful intrigue in their own strongholds, the public school and the polls, especially of our great cities, where a corrupt, irresponsible, secret rule recalls the Council of Ten and the Lion of Saint Mark, and now it is charged that our very legislation at times is not simply partisan but fraudulent. The incompatibility of such proceedings with American principles and American rights recalls with emphatic force the warning so distinctly and repeatedly given us by Dr. Orestes A. Brownson, that eminent and philosophic representative of our citizens of the Roman Catholic faith who stand squarely by the American constitution and American institutions, of the danger of allowing foreigners to meddle with our public schools when he said that American civilization was "the farthest point in advance yet reached by any age or nation, and that foreigners who come to educate according to their civilization necessarily educate for a civilization behind the times and below that of this country."

The enlightening effect of an impartial study of the antislavery contest on an independent and philosophic critic can be read in the interesting and instructive pages of Von Holst; and a review of that contest, from the first presentment of the principles of the Antislavery Society to the parting scene of Grant and Lee at Appomatox, and the adoption of the constitutional amendment of emancipation, affords, step by step, amid whatever mistakes and blunders, evidence which becomes the more striking and conclusive, as time passes, of what was accomplished in the antislavery struggle for humanity and the world in shaping the future of the Republic, by calm resolve, a faithful adhesion to truth and principle, patient perseverance, unflinching courage, faith in the triumph of right, American manliness, and far-sighted Christian statesmanship.

BEDFORD HOUSE, Katonah,
New York, May, 1893.

CONTENTS.

CHAPTER I.

Birth and Education of William Jay.—His Early Philanthropic Interests.—Appointed Judge of Westchester County............ 1

CHAPTER II.

Early Opposition to Slavery.—Growth of the Slave Power.—The Missouri Compromise.—Jay begins Political Agitation for the Abolition of Slavery in the District of Columbia............. 18

CHAPTER III.

Development of the Antislavery Movement.—Organization of Antislavery Societies.—Anti-Abolition Riots.—Jay publishes his "Inquiry"... 39

CHAPTER IV.

Continued Efforts to suppress the Antislavery Movement by Force and Intimidation.—Favourable Effect upon the Public Mind produced by Jay's Writings............................... 63

CHAPTER V.

Gradual Decline of Riotous Demonstrations against the Abolitionists.—Changes occur in the Doctrines and Methods of the American Antislavery Society.—Judge Jay resigns his Membership, while continuing his Efforts on Behalf of Emancipation... 82

CHAPTER VI.

Judge Jay continues to support the Antislavery Cause by his Advice and Writings.—In Consequence of his Opinions he is deprived of his Seat on the Bench.—His Visit to Europe.—His Views on the Liberty Party.—On the Annexation of Texas.—His "Review of the Mexican War."—His Advocacy of International Arbitration as a Remedy for War.—His Work in the Episcopal Church.. 112

CHAPTER VII.

Unpopularity of the Abolitionists.—The Compromises of 1850 and the Fugitive-Slave Law.—Jay's Reply to Webster's 7th of March Speech.—The Attitude of the Episcopal Church.—The Abrogation of the Missouri Compromise.—Disunion 135

CHAPTER VIII.

Death of Judge Jay.—His Position among Antislavery Men.—His other Public and Philanthropic Interests.—His Private Life.—His Character.. 156

Bibliography.. 171

Index... 175

Appendix.. 184

WILLIAM JAY.

CHAPTER I.

BIRTH AND EDUCATION OF WILLIAM JAY.—HIS EARLY PHILANTHROPIC INTERESTS.—APPOINTED JUDGE OF WESTCHESTER COUNTY.

WILLIAM JAY, the second son of John Jay, the first Chief-Justice of the United States, and his wife, Sarah Van Brugh Livingston, was born in the city of New York the 16th of June, 1789. New York was then the seat of the Federal Government, and the year is memorable as that in which the National Constitution superseded the Articles of Confederation, while the inauguration of Washington marked a new era in American history.

During the absence of John Jay in England, while negotiating the "Jay treaty," he was elected Governor of New York, and returned home to assume that office in 1795.

William, then eight years old, was placed at school with the Rev. Thomas Ellison, the rector of St. Peter's Church, Albany. There he received an old-fashioned training. In 1801 he wrote to his father: "Mr. Ellison put me in Virgil, and I can now say the first two eclogues by heart, and construe and parse and scan them." And later on: "I learn nothing but Latin." Among his schoolmates was J. Fenimore Cooper, who afterwards drew a portrait of their old instructor in one of his "Sketches of England," addressed to Jay:

"Thirty-six years ago you and I were schoolfellows and classmates in the house of a clergyman of the true English school. This man was an epitome of the national prejudices and in some respects of the national character. He was the son of a beneficed clergyman in England, had been regularly graduated at Oxford and admitted to orders ; entertained a most profound reverence for the King and the nobility ; was not backward in expressing his contempt for all classes of dissenters and all ungentlemanly sects ; was particularly severe on the immoralities of the French Revolution, and though eating our bread, was not especially lenient to our own ; compelled you and me to begin Virgil with the eclogues, and Cicero with the knotty phrase that opens the oration in favour of the poet Archias, 'because these writers would not have placed them first in the books if they did not intend people to read them first'; spent his money freely and sometimes that of other people ; was particularly tenacious of the ritual and of all the decencies of the Church ; detested a democrat as he did the devil; cracked his jokes daily about Mr. Jefferson, never failing to place his libertinism in strong relief against the approved morals of George III., of several passages in whose history it is charitable to suppose he was ignorant; prayed fervently on Sunday, and decried all morals, institutions, churches, manners, and laws but those of England from Monday to Saturday."

Still, Jay and Cooper were indebted to Ellison's thoroughness in the classics for much of the mental training, the correct taste, and the pure English which marked their subsequent intellectual efforts.

Jay was prepared for college by Henry Davis, afterwards president of Hamilton College. The boy as he appeared at this time was thus described by his cousin, Susan Sedgwick: "As I look back to that fresh spring-time of life, there rises clearly before me a vigorous, sturdy boy, full of health and animation, with laughing eyes, cheeks glowing and dimpled, and exhibiting already marked traits: with a strong will, yet easily reduced by rightful authority; in temper quick, even to passion, but never vindictive; the storm easily raised as soon appeased, thus foreshadowing him at that later period, when, however capable of self-control, his fearless resistance to wrong and uncompromising advocacy of right partook of the same vehement character, happily expressed by his friend, Mr. Fenimore Cooper, who, in reference to his then recently published denunciation of the evils of war, addressed him playfully, 'Thou most pugnacious man of peace.'"

William entered Yale College in January, 1804, in

his fifteenth year. Upon the college roll during his four years were names afterwards well known in our history. There were trained side by side boys who were soon to be arrayed against each other in religion, politics, and in the momentous conflict of slavery with freedom, which, passing from the senate to the field, their sons and grandsons were to terminate by the sword. From the State of South Carolina came John C. Calhoun, who significantly chose for the subject of his graduating oration, "The Qualifications Necessary for a Perfect Statesman;" Christopher Edward Gadsden, afterwards bishop of his native State; and Thomas Smith Grimké, eminent at the bar, in scholarship and philanthropy. Among the Northern students was the Rev. John Pierpont, known as the reformer and poet, who at the age of seventy-six went to the front during the Civil War as chaplain of a Massachusetts regiment; Hon. Henry Randolph Storrs, of New York, the jurist; Rev. Dr. Nathaniel William Taylor, of the Calvinistic school of Edwards and Dwight; Dr. Thomas H. Gallaudet, of Huguenot descent, who devoted himself to the education of deaf-mutes; Dr. Alexander H. Stevens, of New York; Rev. Dr. Samuel Farmer Jarvis, the learned professor of oriental literature; Rev. Dr. Gardiner Spring, of New York, the famous Presbyterian divine; the Hon. William Huntington, of Connecticut; Jacob Sutherland, of New York; and James A. Hillhouse, of New Haven, one of the most scholarly of our poets, whose generous hospitality at his beautiful home, Sachem's Wood, with its avenue of stately elms planted by his father and himself, was for many years the delight of his friends. At Yale Jay met Cooper again, and strengthened a friendship which lasted through life. It was during a visit at Bedford, about 1825, while sitting on the piazza with Chief-Justice Jay, smoking and talking of the incidents of the Revolution, that Fenimore Cooper learned the adventures of a patriotic American, who was apparently attached to the royal cause, but who constantly warned of danger the Continental Army in Westchester and was especially useful during the sitting of the State convention at White Plains. The services and escapes of this man were reproduced in "Harvey Birch, the Spy of the Neutral Ground," which achieved so great a success at home and in Europe, where it still holds its place, having been honoured by more translations, including the Persian and Arabic, than any similar work written in English until the appearance of "Uncle Tom's Cabin."

In a letter to his grandson, William Jay, in 1852, Judge Jay gave some particulars of his college course, which show the simplicity of life in those days and the still lingering influence of English habits: "Through the influence of a professor with whom I had previously lived, I was placed in the room of a resident graduate. The resident graduates were denominated 'Sirs'; they had a pew in the chapel called the Sirs' pew; and when spoken of in college always had Sir prefixed to their names. My room-mate was Sir Holly (Dr. Horace Holly). As a mere freshman I looked up to my room-mate with great respect and treated him accordingly. We had no servants to wait on us, except that a man came every morning to make our beds and sweep the room, and once a week to scatter clean white sand on the floor. I rose early—generally before six in winter—made the fire, and then went, pitcher in hand, often wading through snow, for water for Sir Holly and myself. At that time the freshmen occupied in part the place of sizers in the English universities, and they were required to run errands for the seniors. Our meals were taken in a large hall with a kitchen opening into it. The students were arranged at tables according to their classes. All sat on wooden benches, not excepting the tutors; the latter had a table to themselves on an elevated platform whence they had a view of the whole company. But it was rather difficult for them to attend to their plates and to watch two hundred boys at the same time. Salt beef once a day and dry cod were perhaps the most usual dishes. On Sunday mornings during the winter our breakfast-tables were graced with large tin milk-cans filled with stewed oysters; at the proper season we were occasionally treated at dinner with green peas. As you may suppose, a goodly number of waiters were needed in the hall. These were all students, and many of them among the best and most esteemed scholars. About half-past five in winter the bell summoned us from our beds, and at six it called us to prayers in the chapel. We next repaired to the recitation-rooms and recited by candle-light the lessons we had studied the preceding evening. At eight we had breakfast, and at nine the bell warned us to our rooms. At twelve it called us to a recitation or a lecture. After dinner we recommenced our studies and recited for the third time at four o'clock. During study hours the tutors would frequently go the rounds, looking into our rooms to see that we were not playing truant. Before supper, we all attended evening prayers in the chapel."

The presidency of the college was then occupied by Dr. Timothy Dwight, who also gave instruction in *belles-lettres*, oratory, and theology. To him Jay wrote in 1818: "I retain a grateful recollection of your kind attention to me, and I have, and trust will ever have, reason to acknowledge the goodness of Providence in placing me under your care, when many of my opinions were to be formed and my principles established." Still later, he wrote to a college friend: "Your remarks on Dr. Dwight are grateful to my heart. I cherish his memory as one of the best friends I ever had."

In his senior year Jay took part in debates among the students, presided over by Dr. Dwight. Some of the subjects discussed were: "Ought infidels to be excluded from office?" "Ought religion to be supported by law?" "Would a division of the Union be politic?" "Would it be politic to encourage manufactures in the United States?" On the last question Dr. Dwight remarked: "We shall always buy things where we can get them the cheapest; we will never make our commodities so long as we can buy them better and cheaper elsewhere." Jay displayed his natural inclination for the law by contributing a series of articles on legal subjects, over the signature of "Coke," to the *Literary Cabinet*, the students' paper. He took his degree in September, 1807, having injured his eyesight in his efforts to attain a high standing in his class. "During the winter of my junior year," he wrote in warning to his grandson William, "I was struggling hard for honours, and trying to make up for lost time; I used to rise about four o'clock, light my fire, and sit down to the study of conic sections. I brought on a weakness in my eyes which lasted several years. Be sure you never rise before the sun and study your Latin and Greek by candle-light or gas-light."

After graduation Jay went to Albany and began the study of the law in the office of John B. Henry. On the 3d of September, 1812, he married Augusta, daughter of John McVickar, a merchant of New York, and vestryman of Trinity Church. The difficulty with his eyesight, which had seriously interfered with his legal studies, became so pronounced as to compel him to abandon his profession for some years. During this period he retired with his wife to his father's country seat, "Bedford," in Westchester County, and there devoted himself with energy to agricultural pursuits. The farm included about eight hundred acres, part of a tract purchased by Jacobus van Cortlandt from Katonah Sagamore and other Indian chieftains in 1700, and confirmed by patent of Queen Anne in 1704. It had come to Chief-Justice Jay partly through his mother, Mary van Cortlandt, the wife of Peter Jay, and partly through her sister, Eve van Cortlandt, the wife of Judge John Chambers.

Of the forty fields into which the farm was divided, Jay kept a separate account: showing the tillage and produce, the drainage and fencing, the dates of planting and reaping. A volume of this kind, begun in 1816, contained entries as late as 1857, the year before his death. He perfected himself in grafting and budding, and was particularly successful with peaches, with cherries, pears and plums, some of them with Huguenot names and memories, and with muskmelons from Persian seed, brought to him from the East by a friend. He raised horses from imported stock, Merino sheep, and superintended the curing of hams from a Westphalian recipe, furnished by an old Hessian farm hand—one of the hirelings who had come to conquer and remained to cultivate the country. In 1818 Jay and Fenimore Cooper drafted the constitution for an agricultural society of which Governor Jay was the first president and General Pierre van Cortlandt the second—an institution of great use in the development of Westchester County.

In 1815, when twenty-six years of age, Jay entered upon that course of active philanthropy which for the next forty years employed his thoughts and pen. His first effort was directed to the improvement of his native town of Bedford in the organization of the Society for the Suppression of Vice. By means of this society, of which he was the secretary, he did much to restrain the liquor traffic and to diminish intemperance. Later on, as a judge, he used all the power of the law to the same end; and it was he who suggested the law, still in force, which forbids a tavern-keeper to supply drink on credit.

An interesting incident in this early period of his life was the part which he bore in founding the American Bible Society, in organizing its machinery for the immense work it had to perform, and in vindicating the principles of the society against the attacks of the opposing party in his own church. In this struggle Jay proved the independence of character and courage of conviction which afterwards distinguished him through the seemingly hopeless years of antislavery effort. The general distribution of Bibles in our day makes it difficult to appreciate the limited supply, the high cost, and the consequent rarity of the Bible when this society began its work. The High-Church party in New York were opposed to the association of Episcopalians with other Christians to circulate the Bible, and opposed even to the distribution of the Bible, unless accompanied by the Prayer-book as an interpreter. In these views they were vigorously supported by their distinguished leader, Bishop John Henry Hobart. Jay, who had inherited with his Huguenot blood a faith in the Bible not to be restrained by ecclesiastical assumption, was an officer of the Westchester Bible Society and deeply interested in the work. On the appearance of a pastoral letter from Bishop Hobart in which the High-Church views were expressed, he published a pamphlet showing that it was "the interest and duty of Episcopalians to unite with their fellow-Christians of all denominations in spreading the knowledge of the Word of God." This pamphlet brought him into an active conflict with the eminent bishop which lasted for several years, and taught him that a philanthropic cause, even so plainly meritorious, was not to be carried on without the opposition of powerful conservative interests.

Convinced that a national society could accomplish more than the local and scattered State Bible societies, Jay published a pamphlet in 1816 which showed the imperative importance of the work, and urged united action. At the same time the venerable Elias Boudinot of New Jersey was exerting himself to the same end. When he received a letter from Jay enclosing the pamphlet, he thus welcomed his youthful ally: "These precious moments I have devoted to a full consideration of one of the greatest and most interesting subjects that has ever concerned the children of men. Weak and feeble and scarcely able to think or write, my efforts promised but little in the cause, when your welcome and unexpected letter was brought in. My drooping spirits were raised and my mind greatly revived. I could not help giving glory to God for the great encouragement afforded me to press on in this glorious cause, when I thus beheld His special mercy in raising up so powerful a support in this joyous work and labour of love." In the same year the American Bible Society was formed with the assistance of the best names in the country. Elias Boudinot was chosen president, with John Jay and Matthew Clarkson, a gallant officer of the Revolution, as vice-presidents. Others on the roll were: John Langdon, the statesman of New Hampshire; William Gray, the eminent merchant of Boston; the scholarly John Cotton Smith, of Connecticut, with the blood of the Cottons and the Mathers of colonial history; William Tighlman, the jurist of Pennsylvania; William Wirt and Bushrod Washington, of Virginia; Charles Cotesworth Pinckney, of South Carolina; Governor Worthington, of Ohio; John Bolton, of Georgia; Felix Grundy, of Tennessee; and of New York: Dr. John B. Romeyne; Colonel Richard Varick, Washington's aide; Daniel D. Tompkins, the Governor who obtained the abolition of slavery in the State; John Pintard, John Aspinwall, Jeremiah Evarts, Frederic de Peyster, George Griffin, De Witt Clinton, the Patroon Stephen van Rensselaer, and Colonel Henry Rutgers.

Notwithstanding the honourable support given to the society, it had to resist a carefully organized assault on the part of Bishop Hobart and an influential portion of his clergy aimed at the vital principle on which the success of the movement depended—the cordial union of all Christians. Jay's previous training in the same field of controversy, his staunch devotion at once to his cause and to his church, designated him as the proper person to carry on, in behalf of the society, the war of letters and pamphlets which ensued. Although pitted against an adversary to whom age, experience, and station gave great advantages, he acquitted himself with credit, displaying literary and reasoning powers which were soon to exert a potent effect upon the great moral issue of our time.

Other questions of a philanthropic character occupied his pen. The Synod of Albany having offered a prize for the best essay on the observance of the Sabbath, Jay competed for it with success. A more notable incident of the same sort occurred in 1828. The Savannah Anti-duelling Association offered a medal for the best argument against duelling. The committee appointed to judge the essays were: John Cummings; James M. Wayne, subsequently appointed by President Jackson a justice of the Supreme Court; R. W. Habersham, afterwards Governor of Georgia; William Law; and Matthew Hall McAllister, mayor of Savannah and an opponent of Nullification in 1832. That in 1828 these

Southern men were seeking to root out the habit of duelling, and that the prize should have been awarded by them to William Jay, is a curious commentary on the connection between slavery and duelling. At this time both practices had their opponents at the South who were allowed to express their opinions. As the grip of slavery increased in strength and closed the mouth of every objector, anti-duelling sentiment was simultaneously extinguished. Both barbarous practices were to increase and to perish together. Jay's essay could then find praise among men who a few years later would not tolerate in their homes any product of his pen.

In May, 1818, Jay was appointed one of the judges of Westchester County. The mention of the fact in his diary closed with the words, "May I have grace to discharge with fidelity the duties of the station." Two years later a commission from Governor Clinton made him the first judge of the county, an office which he held until 1823, when the adoption of the new constitution terminated all offices under the old one. Fenimore Cooper then wrote to him, "I see that you are unhorsed with other clever fellows." But in response to a general demand, Governor Clinton reappointed him under the new constitution, and he continued to hold office under successive governors of different parties until 1843, when he was displaced by Governor Bouck at the demand of the pro-slavery wing of the democracy. A decision of Jay's, rejecting a witness who declared his unbelief in God, occurred when De Tocqueville was in the United States, and was commented upon by the distinguished Frenchman as having been accepted by the press without comment, and as showing that the American people combined the notions of Christianity and of liberty so intimately that it was impossible to make them conceive of the one without the other, and that they held religion to be indispensable to the maintenance of republican institutions. In 1862, soon after Jay's death, when an attempt was made by a pro-slavery faction in the county to remove his portrait from the court-house at White Plains, it was defeated by a protest of the members of the bar. "Many of us," they said, "were well acquainted with Judge Jay, and can speak from personal knowledge of those high qualities which have given him an historic celebrity. Whilst he entertained and vigorously vindicated decided opinions on certain questions which have much divided society and produced much acrimony of feeling—in which many of us did not sympathize with him—yet we can all bear testimony to the noble frankness and sincerity of his nature, to his deep interest in all questions tending to advance the interest of the race, and to the extraordinary intellectual strength displayed by him on all occasions in giving expression to his convictions."

In the early years of Jay's life, it appears that his mind turned naturally toward philanthropic subjects. His moral sense was largely developed, his conscience active, his humanity aggressive. His own comfortable circumstances did not close his heart to the sufferings of others. His generous nature longed to replace evil by good. And in the cause which his conscience approved, no obloquy nor social unpopularity could impede his progress. At the same time, there was about him nothing of the intemperate agitator. He was a judge and brought to his philanthropic labours a judicial habit of mind. Indeed, it was this habit of mind which distinguished him among his fellow-workers in the antislavery cause. It was his mission to urge emancipation with the Constitution in his hand; to meet in conflict that portion of society which silenced its uneasy conscience by a repetition of constitutional provisions, and at the same time to combat those who were inclined to seek emancipation by unconstitutional means.

His quiet country life, in which healthful out-of-door pursuits were mingled with the study and reflection of his library, particularly fitted him to look at this all-important question with calmness, with consideration for both sides, and yet with the vigour of a mind free to work exhaustively on a subject involving many conflicting theories and duties. He brought to his task real talents, literary and polemic; a style ready and concise; a reasoning enlivened by an effective vein of irony. He had a refined and benevolent countenance, a pleasing manner, a temper even, but easily roused to indignation at the sight of injustice. Before considering his first connection with the antislavery movement, we may glance at its situation in the early manhood of William Jay.

CHAPTER II.

EARLY OPPOSITION TO SLAVERY.—GROWTH OF THE SLAVE POWER.—THE MISSOURI COMPROMISE.—JAY BEGINS POLITICAL AGITATION FOR THE ABOLITION OF SLAVERY IN THE DISTRICT OF COLUMBIA.

THE movement which culminated in the Civil War and the total abolition of slavery in the United States was first humanitarian, and subsequently political. Philanthropists prepared the way for the statesman and the soldier.

The humanitarian movement had begun before the time of William Jay and his fellow-workers. To find its beginnings, we must look back into the colonial days of the eighteenth century. There, among the first, was George Keith, of Pennsylvania, denouncing the system on grounds of both Christianity and public policy. And Samuel Sewall, Chief-Justice of Massachusetts, who, in his pamphlet, "The Selling of Joseph," quaintly testified to the truth. "These Ethiopians," he said, "as black as they are, seeing they are the sons and daughters of the first Adam and the offspring of God, they ought to be treated with respect agreeable." Ralph Sandiford, Benjamin Lay, William Burling, Anthony

Benezet, the Huguenot, were men who spoke as sincerely as later abolitionists and whose words were heard. There was John Woolman, of New Jersey, who pointed out "the dark gloominess overhanging the land, the spirit of fierceness and love of dominion," resulting from this iniquity; and Dr. Samuel Hopkins, of Newport, R. I., whose eloquent exhortations banished the slave trade from a congregation growing rich on its spoils; and Dr. Benjamin Rush, of Philadelphia, who foretold that "future ages will be at a loss which to condemn most, our folly or our guilt in abetting this direct violation of nature and religion." The legislatures of Virginia, South Carolina, Pennsylvania, and Massachusetts in turn attempted to restrict the slave-trade; but their efforts were annulled in England, where the slave interest, through its champion, Lord Sandwich, forbade any interference with "a traffic so beneficial to the nation."

The colonies had no sooner achieved their independence than they found themselves face to face with the great question, and on the threshold of their national life a great change was perceptible in the attitude of the people towards slavery. The old seventeenth century idea, that to drag a negro from his heathen wilds to labour unrequited in a Christian community tended to the benefit of his soul, had passed away. The slave-trade was generally recognized as indefensible. There were men who denounced slavery itself as an abominable evil. Even those most determined to maintain the institution took the ground that it was an unfortunate necessity, but that it must be preserved to avoid greater evils. In 1787, through the noble efforts of Thomas Jefferson, Timothy Pickering, Rufus King, Nathan Dane, William Grayson, and Richard Henry Lee, Congress passed the great ordinance which forbade slavery to cross the Ohio River into the Northwest Territory.

The struggle between right and wrong had begun, but the opposing forces were very unequal. On one side was humane sentiment; on the other was deeply rooted habit, pecuniary interest, the pressure of political questions of seemingly overriding importance. Among the great leaders of the time there are two whose opinions and practice give an excellent illustration of the prevailing antislavery feeling: John Jay of New York, Patrick Henry of Virginia. There is no disagreement as to the moral elevation of John Jay's character. Abroad and at home, officially and unofficially, he was always the opponent of slavery. Yet Jay purchased and held men as slaves. To obtain domestic servants otherwise was extremely difficult. After his slaves had served him sufficiently long and faithfully to return to him what he considered the value of his outlay, he gave them their freedom. He believed that slavery in principle was wrong, but he yielded so far to convenience and custom. Patrick Henry was an antislavery man and placed his position on record in the following words: "Is it not amazing that, at a time when the rights of humanity are defined and understood with precision, in a country above all others fond of liberty, in such an age, we find men professing a religion the most humane, mild, meek, gentle, and generous adopting a principle as repugnant to humanity as it is inconsistent with the Bible and destructive of liberty? Every thinking, honest man rejects it in speculation, but how few in practice, from conscientious motives! Would any one believe that I am a master of slaves of my own purchase? I am drawn along by the general inconvenience of living without them. I will not, I cannot, justify it; however culpable my conduct, I will so far pay my *devoirs* to duty as to own the excellence and rectitude of her precepts and lament my want of conformity to them. I believe a time will come when an opportunity will be offered to abolish this lamentable evil; everything we can do is to improve it, if it happens in our own day; if not, let us transmit to our own descendants, together with our slaves, a pity for their unhappy lot and an abhorrence of slavery."

Such being the character of antislavery sentiment, its chances of success seem hopeless enough when we hear the other side. When Congress was considering the Articles of Confederation, Wilson, of Pennsylvania, said: "Dismiss your slaves, freemen will take their places." The reply of Lynch, of South Carolina, showed the existence of men willing to sacrifice everything to the preservation of slavery. "Our slaves are our property," said he; "if that is debated, there is an end to confederation."

Thus, at this crisis in the national history, there first distinctively appeared that aggressive, uncompromising party, afterwards to be known as the Slave Power—an association of men then forming a minority even in the South, but determined to carry its point at all hazards; men who were willing to sacrifice every consideration of the public good to the permanence of a system profitable to themselves, but which reduced human beings to the level of beasts. Against a party so resolute, antislavery opinion of the Patrick Henry variety could not prevail. Moreover, the distracted state of the country, the imperative necessity for union, made every other question seem secondary to the majority of patriotic statesmen. In the Constitutional Convention, the Slave Power, then chiefly represented by South Carolina and Georgia, by threatening to defeat the establishment of a stable government and by making the preservation of slavery a *sine qua non* to the Union, obtained the concessions so big with future disaster.

The struggle over this subject in the days of the formation of the government was the beginning of the "irrepressible conflict." The Slave Power had come into being as a distinct force, aiming to dominate the rest of the community in the interest of property in man. On the other hand, the opposition began to organize. Several abolition and manumission societies were formed. The oldest of these was that of Pennsylvania, which in 1787 chose Franklin for its president. A society was formed in New York in 1785 with John Jay as president and Alexander Hamilton as secretary; in Rhode Island in 1789, under the lead of Dr. Hopkins. In 1791, before the Connecticut society, Jonathan Edwards the younger maintained the doctrine of *immediate emancipation*. Similar associations were at work in New Jersey, Virginia, and Maryland. Antislavery men were thus uniting in their cause, but unfortunately they were, with rare exceptions, devoid of the earnestness which characterized their opponents. Their hostility to the system was a sentiment rather than a principle. It could hasten somewhat emancipation at the North; but it had no force to contend against the pecuniary interests which were daily binding tighter the bonds of the negro in the South. There, in the early years of the present century, the cotton-gin, which had been invented in 1793, gave an impetus to the production of cotton which nearly doubled the value of slaves. At the North the profits of the African trade which supplied this increased demand for negroes gave to the Slave Power allies almost as determined as themselves.

The year 1808, fixed by the Constitution as the limit of the duration of the slave-trade, witnessed the next contest. The result was a definite prohibition of the trade by law. But it was a barren victory for the cause of humanity. The interests involved in both Northern and Southern States had grown so large and influential as to make the law a dead letter. The trade continued with unabated vigour, and marked by even greater cruelties to the wretched cargoes. The Slave Power was growing in strength and determination, bent on controlling the national government, influencing our foreign relations, reaching out already to grasp new slave territory.

From 1818 to 1821 continued the great contest over the admission of Missouri as a slave State, in which was involved the question whether the extension and encouragement of slavery was to be the permanent policy of the United States government. Men and words were not wanting to expose and condemn the contemplated evil. But the Slave Power had grown to too great proportions. Henry Clay, who had believed "slavery to be a wrong, a grievous wrong, which no contingency can make right," now, at the behest of slaveholders, threw his great influence against the cause of humanity. As in the days of the Constitutional Convention the Slave Power had secured the perpetuation of its system by threats of preventing a union of the States, so in 1821 it obtained the principle of the extension of slavery by threats of dissolving the Union. Thomas Jefferson, so faithful an advocate of freedom, was now appalled by the sound of a strife which, "like the fire-bell at midnight," announced disaster, and he counselled concession. Even John Quincy Adams was on the same side, "from extreme unwillingness to put the Union in hazard." So passed the so-called Compromise, which allowed slavery to break its bounds and to spread over Arkansas and Missouri. The Slave Power had won a great victory and had shown immense growth. The old apologetic position that the system, although wrong, could not be abolished without entailing greater evils, was now exchanged for the bold doctrine that slavery was a good thing, to be extended and strengthened.

The struggle was growing fiercer and was becoming more clearly an issue between North and South, but the bone of contention was yet the extension, not the abolition, of slavery. The Slave Power, warned by the opposition it had met with in Congress, that a new spirit was arising in the North, instinctively felt that its position could be maintained only by further aggression. None but slaveholders were allowed to represent the South in Congress, where every public measure was considered first in the light of its effect upon the institution of slavery. At home, such humane laws regarding the blacks as still existed were repealed, new and more cruel enactments were passed, the manumission of slaves by grateful or repentant masters was prohibited.

While at the South opinion tended towards united

and vigorous action, the sentiments of the people at the North were divided. The majority, although disliking slavery "in the abstract," were so fearful of the outcome of the contention, were so anxious to see some settlement which would put an end to agitation, that they were disposed to accept the line drawn by the Missouri Compromise as the best solution possible, and to resent any further anti-slavery expression as an element of profitless disturbance. In this class there grew up a dislike of the negroes, a hatred of the questions involved in their existence among us, a general prejudice against colour, which tended greatly to the support of the Slave Power. Many persons who preserved abolition views were lulled into repose of conscience by support of the Colonization Society, an organization formed in the South to get rid of free coloured persons by shipping them to Africa, but skilfully made to appear as a philanthropic scheme to solve the slavery problem. Men of the highest character and with the best intentions had joined this society in the belief that therein might be found the means of uprooting slavery. The ten years following the Missouri Compromise were unpromising for the cause of the slave. The Southern States were ceaselessly strengthening themselves. Race prejudice, the fear of business disturbance, apathy, made the North acquiescent. Cotton was king, and to that authority conscience submitted.

Still there were signs of light and materials for

of a strife which, "like the fire-bell at midnight," announced disaster, and he counselled concession. Even John Quincy Adams was on the same side, "from extreme unwillingness to put the Union in hazard." So passed the so-called Compromise, which allowed slavery to break its bounds and to spread over Arkansas and Missouri. The Slave Power had won a great victory and had shown immense growth. The old apologetic position that the system, although wrong, could not be abolished without entailing greater evils, was now exchanged for the bold doctrine that slavery was a good thing, to be extended and strengthened.

The struggle was growing fiercer and was becoming more clearly an issue between North and South, but the bone of contention was yet the extension, not the abolition, of slavery. The Slave Power, warned by the opposition it had met with in Congress, that a new spirit was arising in the North, instinctively felt that its position could be maintained only by further aggression. None but slaveholders were allowed to represent the South in Congress, where every public measure was considered first in the light of its effect upon the institution of slavery. At home, such humane laws regarding the blacks as still existed were repealed, new and more cruel enactments were passed, the manumission of slaves by grateful or repentant masters was prohibited.

While at the South opinion tended towards united

and vigorous action, the sentiments of the people at the North were divided. The majority, although disliking slavery "in the abstract," were so fearful of the outcome of the contention, were so anxious to see some settlement which would put an end to agitation, that they were disposed to accept the line drawn by the Missouri Compromise as the best solution possible, and to resent any further anti-slavery expression as an element of profitless disturbance. In this class there grew up a dislike of the negroes, a hatred of the questions involved in their existence among us, a general prejudice against colour, which tended greatly to the support of the Slave Power. Many persons who preserved abolition views were lulled into repose of conscience by support of the Colonization Society, an organization formed in the South to get rid of free coloured persons by shipping them to Africa, but skilfully made to appear as a philanthropic scheme to solve the slavery problem. Men of the highest character and with the best intentions had joined this society in the belief that therein might be found the means of uprooting slavery. The ten years following the Missouri Compromise were unpromising for the cause of the slave. The Southern States were ceaselessly strengthening themselves. Race prejudice, the fear of business disturbance, apathy, made the North acquiescent. Cotton was king, and to that authority conscience submitted.

Still there were signs of light and materials for

improvement. In 1822 the exciting struggle for the establishment of slavery in Illinois resulted in favour of freedom. There existed in the country one hundred and forty antislavery societies, of which one hundred and six were in the South. In 1826 was held in Baltimore a convention at which eighty-one of these societies were represented. There was not enough "fight" among these antislavery men to make much impression. Their views were directed towards preventing the extension of slavery, towards its abolition in the District of Columbia (where its existence involved recognition by the United States government) and its "gradual" cessation elsewhere. The fact of their holding the convention in Baltimore indicates the still lingering sympathy of a considerable party in the South, and it shows also that the Slave Power did not look upon them with much concern. It is not until antislavery stands upon the platform of abolition as an *immediate duty* that it is swept from the face of the Southern States.

There were earnest men already engaged in a new and more vigorous crusade: Elias Hicks, the Quaker, who proclaimed boldly the sin of owning men or condoning the practice in others; Rev. John Rankin, of Tennessee, who removed with his congregation across the Ohio River, rather than acquiesce in slavery; William Goodell, of Providence, beginning a career of forty years; above all, Benjamin Lundy, who sacrificed to the cause all that men hold dear. Between 1815 and 1818 four abolition papers were being published, *The Emancipator* in Tennessee, *The Abolition Intelligencer* in Kentucky, *The Liberalist* in Louisiana, and, most important, Lundy's *Genius of Universal Emancipation* in Maryland. All of these papers were published in the South, and the majority of the manumission societies were there. Thus, in 1826, when William Jay began his labours, the line between freedom and slavery was not yet drawn. A few slaves were still held in New York. Many antislavery people were to be found at the South and many pro-slavery people at the North. The United States was a slaveholding nation.

Jay was a deeply interested observer of the contest in Congress which resulted in the Missouri Compromise. In 1819, when he was thirty years of age, his attitude towards the extension of slavery was stated in a letter to Elias Boudinot:

"I have no doubt that the laws of God, and, as a necessary and inevitable consequence, the true interests of our country, forbid the extension of slavery. If our country is ever to be redeemed from the curse of slavery the present Congress must stand between the living and the dead and stay the plague. Now is the accepted time, now is the day of salvation. If slavery once takes root on the other side of the Mississippi, it can never afterwards be extiminated, but will extend with the future Western Empire, poisoning the feelings of humanity, checking the growth of those principles of virtue and religion which constitute alike the security and happiness of civil society."

In the year 1826 occurred an incident which marks the beginning of a new phase in the antislavery struggle—the movement which demanded abolition in the District of Columbia. There, on territory exclusively under the jurisdiction of the National Congress, it could be claimed justly that the question of States rights was not involved and that the constitutional provisions did not apply. In this movement, which continued until its object was accomplished in April, 1862, William Jay was a pioneer.

In August of the year 1826 John Owen, the proprietor of a paper-mill at Croton Falls, near the Jay farm at Bedford, received a parcel from New York which happened to have been wrapped in a Washington newspaper, *The National Intelligencer*, of the 1st of August. On looking it over his eye was caught by the following advertisement:

"Was committed to the jail of Washington County, District of Columbia, on the 22d of July last, a runaway negro man by the name of Gilbert Horton. He is five feet high, stout made, large full eyes, and a scar on his left arm near the elbow; had on when committed a tarpaulin hat, linen shirt, blue cloth jacket and trousers; says that he was born free in the State of New York near Peekskill. The owner or owners of the above-described negro man, if any, are requested to come and take him away, or he will be sold for his jail fees and other expenses, as the law directs."

There is a sort of grim humour about this advertisement, appearing, as it did, according to law, in the capital of the great free republic of the world, under a flag supposed to typify human liberty. It declared that a man who claimed to be and actually was a citizen of the State of New York was held in jail without any charge and would be sold into lifelong slavery unless claimed as a slave by an owner who did not exist. It declared, in short, that a free citizen of the United States who had any negro blood in his veins would be reduced to slavery by the act of setting foot in the capital of his country. Here was an issue which involved the rights of the State of New York, but could not be said to be an attack on those of Virginia or South Carolina.

Mr. Owen recognized in the Gilbert Horton thus described a free man who had worked in his neighbourhood. He lost no time in mounting his horse and riding over to Bedford to submit the matter to Judge Jay. By the latter's advice a letter was despatched at once to the marshal of the District of Columbia, giving proofs of Horton's freedom, and a meeting was called of the citizens of Westchester County to take action on the subject. This meeting, held on the 30th of August, with Oliver Green in the chair and William Jay as secretary, passed the following resolutions:

" I. That this meeting view this procedure with the indignation becoming men who have a just sense of the value of personal liberty, and a proper abhorrence of cruelty and oppression.

"II. That the evidence affords unequivocal proof of the freedom of Horton.

"III. That the secretary is hereby desired to transmit to his Excellency the Governor the evidence above referred to, and, in the name of this meeting, to request his Excellency to demand from the proper authorities the instant liberation of the said Horton as a free citizen of the State of New York.

"IV. That by the fourth article of the Constitution of the United States the citizens of each State are entitled to all the privileges and immunities of the several States, and that it is the duty of the State of New York to protect its citizens in the enjoyment of these rights without regard to their complexion.

"V. That the law under which Horton has been imprisoned, and by which a free citizen without evidence of crime and without trial by jury may be condemned to servitude for life, is repugnant to our republican institutions, and revolting to justice and humanity; and that the representatives of this State in Congress are hereby requested to use their endeavours to procure its repeal.

"VI. That the secretary, with John Owen, Esq., be a committee to prepare and to present to the citizens of this county, for their signatures, a petition to Congress for the immediate abolition of slavery in the District of Columbia.

"VII. That the proceedings of this meeting be signed by the chairman and secretary, and published."

On receiving from Judge Jay the Westchester resolutions, Governor Clinton submitted them immediately to President John Quincy Adams, who was paying a summer visit to his home at Quincy, Mass., with a respectful demand for the liberation of Gilbert Horton as a free man and a citizen. The President sent the papers with a letter from himself to Henry Clay, then Secretary of State. Henry Clay was absent at the time, and the Chief Clerk of the department wrote to Governor Clinton that the instructions of the President had been anticipated by the discharge of Horton by the marshal of the District. The committal had taken place under an old law of Maryland, "which was adopted by Congress with the other general laws then in force in that State for the county of Washington upon its assuming exclusive jurisdiction over the territory."

This disposal of the case left the principle at issue untouched, and Jay could not be satisfied with such a result. His views are expressed in a letter written in September to Hon. Charles Miner, a member of Congress: "Since I read a resolution introduced by you in relation to slavery in the District of Columbia, the subject has been scarcely absent from my mind, and the late imprisonment in Washington of a citizen of this county afforded an opportunity which I gladly embraced of obtaining an expression of public opinion. I do not entertain the slightest hope that our petition will be favourably received, nor the slightest apprehension that the cause we espouse will not finally triumph. The history of the abolition of the slave-trade teaches us the necessity of patient perseverance, and affords a pledge that perseverance will be ultimately crowned with success. We have nothing to fear, but much to hope, from the violence and threats of our opponents. Apathy is the only obstacle we have reason to dread, and to remove this obstacle it is necessary that the attention of the public should be constantly directed to the subject. Every discussion in Congress in relation to slavery, no matter how great may be the majority against us, advances our cause. We shall rise more powerful from every defeat."

Jay's next step was to draft the memorial to Congress ordered by the Westchester resolutions. It declared:

"The outrage offered to a citizen of this county, and a violation of the constitutional rights involved in that outrage, affords to the meeting new and strong evidences of the impropriety of the continuance of slavery in the District of Columbia. As citizens of the republic, professing to acknowledge that all men are created equal, and that they are endowed by their Creator with certain inalienable rights, and that among them are life, liberty, and the pursuit of happiness, your petitioners cannot but regard it as derogatory to the government of the country that its laws should violate any of these rights in a territory under its exclusive jurisdiction. To your honourable body was given by the Constitution the exclusive jurisdiction in all cases whatever over that District, and your right and ability to grant the prayer of these petitioners cannot be called in question, and the confined limit of the District and the comparatively small number of slaves it contains obviates the objections sometimes urged against sudden emancipation.

"Your petitioners therefore earnestly entreat your honourable body that the government of this great republic, glorying as it does in acknowledging and protecting the rights of mankind, diffusing the blessings of freedom, may no longer by law withhold these rights and blessings from any portion of the inhabitants of its own immediate territory, but in the exercise of your prerogative you will immediately provide for the abolition of slavery in the District of Columbia in such manner as in your wisdom may seem best."

The publication of the Westchester resolutions elicited no unfavourable comments at the North, but it gave no little disquietude to Southern editors, two of whom declared that black persons travelling in the South should carry proofs of their freedom, as whites in Europe were compelled to carry passports. The introduction of the subject into Congress, even at that day, when there was no excitement at the North on the subject of slavery, brought out the susceptibility and dictatorial tone of the slaveholding interest which marked all subsequent debates up to the election of Lincoln.

Soon after the assembling of Congress in 1827, Mr. Aaron Ward, representing Westchester County, introduced the resolution: "That the committee on the District of Columbia be directed to enquire whether there be in force in the said District any law which authorizes the imprisonment of any man of colour and his sale as an unclaimed slave for gaol fees, and if so to enquire into the expediency of repealing the same." Mr. Ward accompanied his resolution with remarks of a moderate character, referring to the circumstances of Horton's arrest, the fact of his being a citizen of New York, and the danger in which he stood of being sold as a slave; he contrasted the law under which such proceedings could be had with the provisions of the national Constitution; and he concluded by saying: "The jurisdiction of the District, sir, ought to be exhibited to the country and to the world without a stain. Its object should be not to oppress but to vindicate the rights of freemen, and if there is a spot on earth where these rights are to be held sacred that place is the District of Columbia."

For a Northern man merely to touch upon the rights of coloured persons was enough to arouse the leading Southern members of the House to angry opposition. John Forsythe, who as minister to Spain had arranged the session of Florida, James Hamilton, already an extreme advocate of States rights and afterwards Governor of South Carolina, Charles A. Wickliffe, afterwards Postmaster-General under President Tyler, and George McDuffie, of Georgia, all took pains to throw ridicule upon the resolution, or to oppose its consideration. They considered, no doubt correctly, that to have any negroes spoken of in Congress otherwise than as property was an indirect blow at slavery. W. L. Brent, of Maryland, said that the resolution as it stood was calculated to excite only angry debate and irritated feelings. If the mover would omit the words "being a citizen of any State," the most objectionable part would be removed. Mr. Ward consented to this emasculation and his resolution was then carried. The committee reported on the 16th July, that in the District of Columbia, "if a free man of colour should be apprehended as a runaway, he is subjected to the payment of all fees and rewards given by law for apprehending runaways; and upon failure to make such payment, is liable to be sold as a slave." "That is," said Judge Jay, "a man acknowledged to be free and unaccused of any offence is to be sold as a slave to pay fees and rewards given by law for apprehending runaways. If Turkish despotism is disgraced by an enactment of equal atrocity, we are ignorant of the fact." The committee thought the law rather hard, and recommended such an alteration of it as would make such charges payable by the corporation of Washington. But even this alteration was never made. "The code of Washington," Jay said some years later, "is yet polluted by unquestionably the most iniquitous statute in Christendom." And the fact continued that a coloured citizen of a free State could be sold into slavery if found in Washington. Convinced that no reform could be expected except by the total abolition of slavery on United States territory, convinced, too, that this was the first necessary step in a campaign against slavery itself, Jay set on foot a movement for popular petitions to Congress and for legislative expression in behalf of their consideration. The Pennsylvania Legislature passed such resolutions in January, 1829; the New York Assembly followed soon afterwards, when Jay wrote to his friend Charles Miner: "The mail this evening brings the news that resolutions instructing our representatives in Congress to vote for the abolition of slavery in the District of Columbia have passed our Assembly by a vote of 57 to 39. In the fulness of my heart I thank God and take courage." Among his co-workers at this time was Henry D. Sedgwick, to whom he wrote in 1831: "I have read your pamphlet with much interest; your ideas on the abolition of slavery correspond with those I have long entertained and expressed. Duty is the only safe rule of expediency. No nation ever has suffered, and none ever will, for doing justice and loving mercy. But moral considerations apart, I have no doubt it would be wise policy in the Southern States immediately to emancipate their slaves. The period must arrive when slavery must cease on this continent. The progress of knowledge and religion, the example of St. Domingo, the abolition of slavery in Mexico and South America, the decreasing value of slave labour, and the rapidly augmenting coloured population in the South, all combine in rendering this event inevitable. But the slaves will either receive their freedom as a boon, or they will wrest it by force from their masters; and the evils attending these two modes of emancipation certainly bear no proportion to each other. You remark, 'Our country fought for justice and should be ready to render the justice which it demanded.' I observe a similar sentiment in a letter written by my father from Spain to Judge Benson during the contest to which you allude. Speaking of the abolition of slavery, he says, 'Till America comes into this measure her prayers to Heaven for liberty will be impious.' This is a strong expression, but it is just. Were I in your Legislature I would prepare a bill for the purpose with great care, and would never cease moving it till it became a law or I ceased to be a member. I believe that God governs the world, and I believe it to be a maxim in His Court, as in ours, that those who ask for equity ought to do it. I do not think the free States guiltless of upholding slavery while, through their representatives, they tolerate it in the District of Columbia. Were the free States to will it, slavery would cease at the capital of the republic, and an example would be set that could not fail of having a salutary influence."

CHAPTER III.

DEVELOPMENT OF THE ANTISLAVERY MOVEMENT.—ORGANIZATION OF ANTISLAVERY SOCIETIES.—ANTI-ABOLITION RIOTS.—JAY PUBLISHES HIS "INQUIRY."

CHIEF-JUSTICE JAY died at Bedford in 1828, and his son William occupied his leisure during the following five years in preparing " The Life and Letters of John Jay." This work was published in two octavo volumes in 1833, and was highly praised for both thoroughness and impartiality.

Meanwhile events were occurring which raised antislavery sentiment from the torpor in which it had fallen after the excitement of the Missouri Compromise, and which brought the whole question before the people as a live issue which compelled attention. Between the years 1829 and 1832 took place a remarkable series of debates in Virginia on the subject of slavery, brought about by dissatisfaction with the State constitution and by the Nat Turner massacre, in which a number of slaves had risen against their masters. In these debates the evils of slavery were exposed as clearly as they were afterwards by the Abolitionists, and with an outspoken freedom which, when indulged in by Northern men, was soon to be denounced as treasonable and incendiary. These Southern speakers were silenced by the Slave Power. But there were men in the North who thought the same and who would not be silenced. Chief among these was William Lloyd Garrison. He had begun his memorable career by circulating petitions in Vermont in 1828 in favor of emancipation in the District of Columbia. Having joined Lundy in Baltimore in editing the *Genius of Universal Emancipation*, he had suffered ignominy in the cause in a Southern jail; drawing from persecution and hardship only new inspiration, he began the publication of the *Liberator* at Boston in January, 1831. In the following year, under his leadership, was formed the New England Anti-Slavery Society, which placed itself on the new ground that *immediate, unconditional emancipation, without expatriation, was the right of every slave and could not be withheld by his master an hour without sin*. In March, 1833, the *Weekly Emancipator* was established in New York, with the assistance of Arthur and Lewis Tappan, and under the editorship of William Goodell. In the same year appeared at Haverhill, Mass., a vigorous pamphlet by John G. Whittier, entitled "Justice and Expediency, or Slavery considered with a View to its Rightful and Effectual Remedy, Abolition." Nearly simultaneously were published Mrs. Lydia Maria Child's "Appeal in Behalf of that Class of Americans called Africans," and a pamphlet by Elizur Wright, Jr., a professor in the Western Reserve College, on "The Sin of Slavery and its Remedy."

These publications and the doctrines of the *Liberator* produced great excitement throughout the country. The South had been able to hear the words "gradual emancipation" with a confident equanimity, and only a few years before had tolerated a convention in Baltimore gathered to forward that object. But the word "immediate" now prefixed to emancipation acted as a firebrand to gunpowder. Southern newspapers and politicians could not find epithets strong enough to denounce the fanatical incendiaries who said that slavery, being wrong in itself, should cease at once. A reward was offered by a Southern Legislature for the person of Garrison, dead or alive. For lending Whittier's pamphlet to a white man Dr. Reuben Crandall was tried for his life at Washington on the charge of "circulating Tappan, Garrison & Co.'s papers encouraging the negroes to insurrection."

The lives of the abolitionists were safer at the North, but their principles were condemned there in terms quite as decided. To say that slavery ought to be immediately abolished was sufficient cause for the clergyman to lose his pulpit and the merchant his credit. The new doctrine was too sound to be ignored, and its agitation was disorganizing, vexatious, injurious to business, destructive of private and political peace. The North agreed with the South that slavery was not a subject to which the right of free speech applied. The abolitionists were accused of injuring the cause of the blacks by their proceedings. And indeed, at the South the treatment of the slave became harsher, and at the North the prejudice against the free negro was intensified. In 1833 Miss Crandall, a Quaker lady, endeavoured to establish a boarding-school for the education of coloured girls in Canterbury, Conn. A committee of the inhabitants waited upon her, who represented "that by putting her design into execution she would bring ruin and disgrace upon them all." Three town meetings were held in one week to discuss ways and means to suppress a scheme which would render "insecure the persons, property, and reputation of our citizens." The State of Connecticut passed a special law to forbid the establishment of such a school. Under it, Miss Crandall was tried and convicted. The constitutionality of the law was called in question and the case was appealed. But the inhabitants of Canterbury thought the crisis too serious to depend on legal technicalities. Miss Crandall was driven from the town by persecution. The shops would sell her no food; her well was filled with manure, and water from other sources refused; her house was smeared with filth and finally set on fire. The trustees of the Noyes Academy in Plymouth, N. H., having consented to the admission of coloured pupils, the respectable people of the town avoided the contemplated disgrace by moving the school building from its foundations and depositing it in a swamp. In 1835 a wealthy coloured man bought a pew on the floor of Park Street Church in Boston. His neighbours nailed up the door of the pew, and so many "aggrieved brethren" threatened to leave that the trustees were obliged to prevent the threatened contamination of the sanctuary by excluding the coloured pew-holder. A hundred similar cases might be cited to show that before the emancipation of the slaves could gain even a hearing, the North had to be educated to consider the negro race as human beings capable of improvement and deserving of humane encouragement.

In May, 1833, Judge Jay contributed to the first number of the *Emancipator* a letter which sets forth his own views of the problem of American slavery at that time and also some of the difficulties in the path of the emancipationists:

"The duty and policy of immediate emancipation, although clear to us, are not so to multitudes of good people who abhor slavery and sincerely wish its removal. They take it for granted, no matter why or wherefore, that if the slaves were now liberated they would instantly cut the throats and fire the dwellings of their benefactors. Hence these good people look upon the advocates of emancipation as a set of dangerous fanatics, who are jeopardizing the peace of the Southern States and riveting the fetters of the slaves by the very attempt to break them. In their opinion the slaves are not fit for freedom, and therefore it is necessary to wait patiently till they are. Now, unless these patient waiters can be brought over to our side, emancipation is hopeless; for, first, they are an immense majority of all among us who are hostile to slavery; and, secondly, they are as conscientious in their opinions as we are in ours, and unless converted will oppose and defeat all our efforts. But how are they to be converted? Only by the exhibition of Truth. The moral, social, and political evils of slavery are but imperfectly known and considered. These should be portrayed in strong but true colours, and it would not be difficult to prove that, however inconvenient and dangerous emancipation may be, the continuance of slavery must be infinitely more inconvenient and dangerous.

"Constitutional restrictions, independent of other considerations, forbid all other than moral interference with slavery in the Southern States. But we have as good and perfect a right to exhort slaveholders to liberate their slaves as we have to exhort them to practice any virtue or avoid any vice. Nay, we have not only the right, but under certain circumstances it may be our duty to give such advice; and while we confine ourselves within the boundaries of right and duty, we may and ought to disregard the threats and denunciations by which we may be assailed.

"The question of slavery in the District of Columbia is totally distinct, as far as we are concerned, from that of slavery in the Southern States.

"As a member of Congress, I should think myself no more authorized to legislate for the slaves of Virginia than for the serfs of Russia. But Congress has full authority to abolish slavery in the District, and I think it to be its duty to do so. The public need information respecting the abominations committed at Washington with the sanction of their representatives—abominations which will cease whenever those representatives please. If this subject is fully and ably pressed upon the attention of our electors, they may perhaps be induced to require pledges from candidates for Congress for their votes for the removal of this foul stain from our National Government. As to the Colonization Society, it is neither a wicked conspiracy on the one hand nor a panacea for slavery on the other. Many good and wise men belong to it and believe in its efficacy."

In the summer of 1833 the abolitionists of Great Britain succeeded in obtaining the act of emancipation for the 800,000 slaves in the West Indies. In June Arthur Tappan wrote to Judge Jay asking for his "opinion as to the expediency of forming an American Antislavery Society and of doing it now. The impulse given to the cause by the movement in England would, it appears to me, aid us greatly here." Jay replied very cautiously. A New York society, he thought, might be desirable immediately. The constitutions and proceedings of such societies demanded great caution and prudence; they must blend the wisdom of the serpent with the harmlessness of the dove. The Southern people affected to apprehend an unconstitutional interference with their property, as they called it, by the Northern abolitionists, and no ground for such pretended fear should be given. With this view, he suggested the incorporation into the constitution of antislavery societies a distinct declaration, such as the following: "We concede that Congress, under the present National Compact, has no right to interfere with any of the slave States in relation to this momentous subject. But we maintain that Congress has a right and is solemnly bound to suppress the domestic slave-trade between the several States and to abolish slavery in those portions of our territory which the Constitution has placed under its exclusive jurisdiction." He further suggested that the two subjects, the Colonization Society and the political condition of the free blacks, should be avoided. "Duty and policy," he said, "in my opinion demand the emancipation of our slaves, but they do not demand that immediately on their emancipation they shall be invested with the right of suffrage."

On the 2d of October the New York City Antislavery Society was successfully organized, despite an active and organized effort to prevent it. A call had been issued for a meeting of the friends of immediate emancipation at Clinton Hall. A counternotice was published, signed "Many Southerners," inviting a meeting at the same time and place. The proprietors of Clinton Hall, alarmed at the situation, refused to let it to the abolitionists, who then applied to the Clinton Hotel, where they were also refused. The Southerners and their Northern sympathizers, finding Clinton Hotel closed, held a meetting at Tammany Hall, with General Bogardus, the United States Marshal, in the chair, with speeches and resolutions against the abolitionists, when a report that the abolitionists were in session at Chatham Street Hall sent them there in haste, only to find the Hall closed and dark. An eye-witness described the crowd assembled by the Southern call as "a genuine drunken, infuriated mob of blackguards of every species, some with good clothes, and the major part the very sweepings of the city." The public was amused the next morning by a leading editorial in the *Courier and Enquirer*, congratulating the country on the failure of the "disorganizing fanatics to organize a society fraught with danger to the Union and based upon an open violation of the United States Constitution;" while the advertising column of the same sheet contained the official proceedings of the abolitionists at the Chatham Street Chapel, where with promptness, energy, and order they had received the report of a committee, adopted a constitution, elected officers, adjourned and closed the building before the arrival of the rioters from Tammany. The successful management of the affair was due chiefly to the coolness and skill of Lewis Tappan, to whose devotion and energy the antislavery cause was from this time constantly indebted. The peaceful and lawful aims of the society, its frank acknowledgment of the rights of the Southern States were set forth in its constitution:

"While it admits that each State in which slavery exists has, by the Constitution of the United States, the exclusive right to legislate in regard to its abolition in said State, it shall aim to convince all our fellow-citizens, by arguments addressed to their understandings and consciences, that slaveholding is a heinous crime in the sight of God, and that the duty, safety, and best interest of all concerned require its immediate abandonment, without expatriation. The society will also endeavour in a constitutional way to influence Congress to put an end to the domestic slave-trade and to abolish slavery in all those portions of our common country which come under its control, especially in the District of Columbia, and likewise to prevent the extension of it to any State that may hereafter be admitted to the Union.

"The society shall aim to elevate the character and condition of the people of colour, by encouraging their intellectual, moral, and religious improvement, and by removing public prejudice, that thus they may *according to their intellectual and moral worth* share an equality with the whites of civil and religious privileges; but this society will never in any way countenance the oppressed in vindicating their rights by resorting to physical force."

Notwithstanding the distinct and moderate language in which the society set forth its lawful objects, pro-slavery prejudice was aroused to violent opposition. A week later a meeting was called to protest against the "reckless agitations of the abolitionists." Theodore Frelinghuysen, United States Senator from New Jersey, declared that "nine tenths of the horrors of slavery were imaginary," that "the crusade of abolition" was "the poetry of philanthropy," that emancipationists were "seeking to dissolve the Union." Chancellor Walworth came down from Albany to say that they were "reckless incendiaries" and their efforts unconstitutional. David B. Ogden declared the doctrine of immediate emancipation to be "a palpable and direct nullification of the Constitution."

On the 29th of October, 1833, a circular invitation was addressed to Judge Jay and others to attend a convention at Philadelphia on the 4th December to form a National Antislavery Society. This step was taken in concurrence with the views of the friends of immediate emancipation in Boston, Providence, New York, and Philadelphia. Among the motives for organizing such a society without delay it was argued that union is strength; that the advocates of the immediate abolition of slavery, though comparatively few and much scattered, were many in the aggregate, and could act, when combined, with irresistible power; that the cause was urgent, public expectation excited, its friends to some extent committed to such a movement during the present year; that they had the example of similar organizations, which, though feeble and condemned by public opinion in the outset, had speedily risen to great influence, and had been the means under God of immense benefit to the human race, especially in the case of the National Antislavery Society of Great Britain, and of the American Temperance Society. The invitation was signed by a committee consisting of Arthur Tappan, Joshua Leavitt, and Elizur Wright, Jr., all officers of the New York Antislavery Society.

At the same time Judge Jay received a letter from

Rev. Samuel J. May urging him to be present. "This is a cause," wrote May, "in which our wisest and best and most prudent men ought to engage. There never has been in our country so great a demand for the exertions of true patriots and real Christians. . . . Let me beg of you to be there, at the convention. I have heard the hope that you will be there expressed most fervently by many."

Jay replied to the committee that he could not be present. "It would perhaps be uncandid to conceal from you," he said, "that the expediency of the proposed attempt to form a National Society at the present time seems to me to be at least questionable. May it not increase the irritation and hostility extensively felt towards abolitionists without promoting their objects more effectually than local societies? If, however, a National Society is to be formed, it is to be hoped its proceedings will be marked with great prudence and moderation. The great objection made to antislavery associations is that they aim at an unconstitutional interference with slavery. This objection, false as I am persuaded it is, has nevertheless an extensive and injurious influence, and unless it be removed success will be hopeless. It seems to me, therefore, of the utmost importance that correct constitutional principles on this subject should not only be entertained, but explicitly and unequivocally avowed by every antislavery society. This avowal might be made in the preamble of their constitution in some form like the following:

"'The object of this society is to promote the abolition of slavery in the United States. As all legislation relative to slavery in the several States in which it exists can be constitutionally exercised only by their respective Legislatures, this society will endeavour to effect its object, so far as relates to these States, by argument addressed to the understanding and conscience of their citizens. But inasmuch as the Federal Constitution confers on Congress the exclusive right to legislate for the District of Columbia, this society will use all such lawful and constitutional means as may be deemed advisable to induce Congress to abolish slavery in that District without delay.'

"I am very sensible that the friends of emancipation hold these principles, but not having given them sufficient prominence in their writings they have subjected themselves to much injurious suspicion."

Judge Jay's letter was read on the first day of the Antislavery Convention held in Philadelphia in December, 1833; and in the declaration of principles, reported by William Lloyd Garrison, John G. Whittier, and Samuel J. May, and unanimously adopted by the convention, appeared the following clauses, by which the abolitionists were enabled to repel the charge, so persistently made, that they sought to accomplish their ends by unconstitutional means, by asking Congress to exceed its power by meddling with slavery in the States:

"We fully and unanimously recognize the sovereignty of each State to legislate exclusively on the subject of slavery which is tolerated within its limits; we concede that Congress under the present National Compact has no right to interfere with any of the slave States in relation to this momentous subject.

"But we maintain that Congress has a right and is solemnly bound to suppress the domestic slave-trade between the several States, and to abolish slavery in those portions of our territory which the Constitution has placed under its exclusive jurisdiction."

In 1838 an energetic attempt was made by Alvan Stewart, of Utica, to strike out the clause in the constitution of the American Antislavery Society which recognized the rights of the Southern States under the United States Constitution. Jay perceived the injury that such a course would inflict on the position of the abolitionists. It would, indeed, have committed the society to the doctrine that Congress could continue slavery in the States. He opposed the change with vigour during a debate of two days and succeeded in maintaining the all-important clause.

Looked at by the light of subsequent events, the importance of placing the antislavery movement on a strictly constitutional basis cannot be overrated. Upon the principles thus distinctly avowed rested the moral and political strength of the movement during a struggle of nearly thirty years. And these principles became, in 1854, under the guidance of the founders of the Republican party, the chief plank in the platform of that great organization, under whose sturdy lead, aided by citizens of all parties, the supremacy of the national Constitution was maintained, the integrity of the national territory was preserved, slavery was ended, and the republic saved.

Judge Jay was not yet officially connected with the antislavery societies, but his sympathy was close with them and their officers. At the request of the Executive Committee of the New York society, he drafted a petition for abolition in the District of Columbia for circulation in New York, in which he again distinctly drew the line between the power of Congress over the District and its want of power as regarded the States. This careful discrimination had no weight with the many who were unwilling to admit that anything said or done by the abolitionists was right. But it succeeded with more liberal men, among them the good Chancellor Kent. The Chancellor, whose reputation as a jurist was second to none, signed the petition, which he declared to contain "no unconstitutional doctrine."

The first anniversary of the American Antislavery Society was held at the Chatham Street Chapel in the beginning of May, 1834. Arthur Tappan presided, and addresses were made by Elizur Wright, Jr., Rev. Amos A. Phelps of Boston, James A. Stone of Kentucky, a delegate from the Lane Seminary, Robert Purvis of Philadelphia, Rev. Henry G. Ludlow, Wm. Lloyd Garrison, and Charles Stewart. The meeting met with disorderly interruptions; the newspapers contained abusive attacks upon the abolitionists and appealed against them to the passions of the lowest and most ignorant class in the community. "All this violence and obloquy," remarked Judge Jay, "are not without an object, and that object is intimidation." The truth of this observation was soon disgracefully verified. When the Fourth of July was celebrated at the Chatham Street Chapel by an antislavery oration from David Paul Brown of Philadelphia, the disorderly elements evoked by the press against the blacks and abolitionists responded in large force and with increased lawlessness. On the 9th of July a mob assembled at the Chapel, broke open the doors, passed resolutions in favor of the Colonization Society and by a suggestive vote adjourned until the next meeting of the Antislavery Society. The mob then proceeded to the Bowery Theatre to avenge some expressions attributed to an English actor, and next to the house of Mr. Lewis Tappan, which was attacked with bricks and stones, the furniture broken up and burned in the street. The riots continued for several days with little hindrance from the city authorities. Six churches were attacked and a large number of houses occupied by abolitionists or by coloured people. Against the latter the fury of the mob was especially directed. The same scenes of riot and cruelty toward the helpless blacks occurred in Philadelphia, where forty-five houses were destroyed. It was evident that the arguments of the abolitionists could not be met except with violence. The mobs, as usual, were cowardly. In some cases the determined action of the abolitionists afforded them the protection refused by the police. It was announced that among the houses to be attacked was that of Dr. Abraham L. Cox, in Broome Street, a few doors east of Broadway. John Jay, then a student at Columbia College, was living in the house. Some members of the New York Young Men's Antislavery Society, with guns and pistols, were gathered within and notice was given publicly that an attack would be repelled by force. Late that night the mob in its lawless career passed close to Dr. Cox's house, but did not dare to molest it. Similar preparations for defence saved the store of Arthur Tappan.

While the New York mob, as the *Commercial Advertiser* said, were "now nightly engaged in deeds of violence," the same paper distinctly took the ground that the abolitionists should not enjoy "the protection of the law and the aid of the military," except "on condition that the causers of these mischiefs shall be abated and the outrages upon public feelings from the forum, the pulpit, and the press shall no more be repeated by these reckless incendiaries." The *Courier and Inquirer* of the same day said: "Now we tell them [the abolitionists] that when they openly and publicly promulgate doctrines which outrage public feelings, they have no right to demand protection of the people they insult," and they must understand "that they prosecute their treasonable and beastly plans at their own peril."

Such was the view taken of American freedom of speech by the pro-slavery party. The manly traits of American character seemed to be lost in the prevailing atmosphere of race prejudice, cowardice, and injustice. Politicians of both parties, representatives of the commercial and professional classes of the North, acquiesced in a policy which they thought would advance their views, but which was destructive of the fundamental principles of American liberty. The highest and the lowest had joined hands to assail the coloured people and their friends. Names honoured in the Church and the State, which should have helped to elevate public opinion and to guide it in the path of justice, obeyed the mandates and echoed the denunciations of the Slave Power. For a time was presented an alliance in behalf of slavery of the highest classes with the scum of politicians and criminals. The intrepid William Leggett was one of the few who dared to publish the truth. "The fury of demons," he wrote in the *Evening Post*, "seems to have entered into the breasts of our misguided populace. The rights of public and private property, the obligations of law, the authority of its ministers and even the power of the military are all equally spurned by these audacious sons of riot and disorder." Candid and cautious thinkers began to take alarm at the disregard for law which seemed to be spreading through the country. "These mobs," wrote Dr. Channing, "are indeed most dishonourable to us as a people, because they have been too much the expression of public sentiment, . . . because there was a willingness that the antislavery movement should be put down by force."

The conduct of the mobs, and the encouragement given to them by the press, aroused the spirit and stimulated the energy of the abolitionists. "These crimes," said Judge Jay, "abundantly prove the extreme cruelty and sinfulness of that prejudice against colour which we are impiously told is an ordination of Providence. Colonizationists, assuming the prejudice to be natural and invincible, propose to remove its victims beyond its influence. Abolitionists, on the contrary, remembering with the Psalmist 'that it is He that hath made us, and not we ourselves,' believe that the benevolent Father of us all requires us to treat with justice and kindness every portion of the human family."

Although he had been an earnest emancipationist for ten years, Judge Jay had had doubts of the wisdom of forming antislavery societies at so early a period in the movement. He had feared that unmeasured and unconstitutional doctrines might be adopted which would set the cause in a false light before the country. His advice had been sought and followed, as we have seen, and there was no longer any reason why he should not become an active member. In 1834, immediately after the riots and when the outlook seemed darkest, he took a place on the Executive Committee of the National Society.

"In that season of feverish excitement," wrote

Hon. Henry Wilson, "Judge William Jay, inheriting not only the honoured name, but the principles and purity of the illustrious Chief-Justice, at first declined an office in the new society, deeming its organization premature," but now "sought to take his share of its labours and responsibilities. His name gave prestige; his talents, learning, and integrity afforded strength, while his cautious and ready pen laid precious gifts upon its altar."

In February, 1835, was published Jay's "Inquiry into the Character and Tendency of the American Colonization and American Antislavery Societies." The book bore upon its title-page the words of Milton, "Give me liberty to know, to utter, and to argue freely, according to my conscience, above all liberties"—a sentiment considered treasonable in America by the Slave Power. This work had a powerful effect upon public opinion, not only on account of the arguments it contained, but largely on account of the character and position of its author. It was the policy of the pro-slavery party to represent the abolitionists as ignorant and reckless agitators, with nothing to lose. But here was a man of family and fortune, a judge on the bench, high in the counsels of the Episcopal Church, who set forth the detested doctrines with judicial moderation and unanswerable logic.

Jay began by an exposure of the Colonization Society. He showed that it was merely a scheme to get rid of the free blacks at the South, where they were regarded as a nuisance; that its officers represented it at the North as a solution of the slavery question to quiet emancipationists and to obtain their subscriptions. He set forth the constitutional and merciful objects of the American Antislavery Society. He showed that abolitionists were neither acting in opposition to law, nor were in any manner exciting the slaves to insurrection; that the opinions they professed were such as had been freely uttered by Jefferson, Franklin, and numerous Southern statesmen within fifty years. He exposed the cruel character of American slavery, the beastly degradation, physical, moral, and mental, to which it condemned the blacks; the horrors of the interstate slave-trade, tearing husband from wife and children from their mothers to be sold into distant places; he pointed out the national disgrace involved in the fact that in the city of Washington, under the stars and stripes, slave-dealers were licensed to ply their trade in human flesh, leading the chained "coffles" of black wretches about the streets. The concluding chapters were devoted to showing that emancipation could be accomplished with safety, and that the real danger to the country lay in the continuation of slavery.

The welcome extended to this book by the avowed abolitionists is illustrated by the following extract from the annual report of the Massachusetts Antislavery Society in 1836: "We know it will not be thought invidious towards others who have greatly contributed by their excellent writings to help on our glorious enterprise, if we make especial mention of the volume from the pen of the Hon. William Jay of New York. His 'Inquiry' was published in the early part of last year. Coming from him, a man extensively known, and highly respected and beloved by all who know him, it could not fail to command the public attention. The very rapid sale of the first and second editions evinced the eagerness of thousands to know the results of his inquiry into the sentiments and plans of the two societies which had stood from the birth of the latter in the attitude of opposition. It is a book so full of pertinent facts and carefully drawn conclusions that it could not fail to impart the convictions of its author to other minds. No book on the subject has probably been read by more persons, nor has any one been instrumental to the conversion of more."

The importance of the "Inquiry" to the antislavery cause is illustrated by the diverse character of the men whose attention was attracted by it— men whose conservative habits of mind, whose business and professional interests caused them to ignore if not to condemn the abolitionists. "Your book," wrote Rev. Beriah Green, who presided at the organization of the American Antislavery Society in Philadelphia, "will command a large circle of readers who could not be persuaded to examine a paragraph written by any of us who have so long been known and hated and execrated as abolitionists.

To many of these, your arguments, so skilfully arranged, so powerfully described, so happily conducted to so triumphant a conclusion, must prove convincing. They must abandon their 'miry clay,' and, aided by your hand, take a position 'on the rock.'" Among leading men influenced by Jay's "Inquiry" may be mentioned Dr. Alonzo Potter, afterwards Bishop of Pennsylvania, and Peter G. Stuyvesant, a representative of the solid Knickerbockers of New York. Edward Delavan, of Albany, wrote: "You have done the cause of humanity an incalculable amount of good by the work." Mrs. Theodore Sedgwick wrote from Stockbridge: "We are reading your book on American slavery with great interest. You have rendered an invaluable service to the country and to the cause of humanity." The approbation most welcome to Jay was probably that of the eminent Chancellor Kent. "I have read the volume," he said, "with equal interest and astonishment. You have accumulated a mass of facts of which a great part were to me unknown, and they are of a surprising kind. I do not well see how your argument on any material point can be gainsaid. You have amply vindicated the character and intentions of the American Antislavery Society from all injurious imputations. The details of the slave-trade and its accompanying atrocities, as carried on at Washington, are horrible, and your work must go far towards opening the eyes and disabusing the minds of the public. I have, from the very beginning, had doubts and misgivings as to the efficacy and results of the American Colonization Society, and for some years past I have become satisfied that the scheme was in reality but an Utopian vision, though I had supposed until now that its fruits were better. Permit me to add that I have been much pleased, not only with the clearness, force, simplicity, and precision of the style, but with your fearless, frank, and manly, but courteous vindication of the cause of Truth and Justice, and with your striking appeals to the conscience and responsibilities of the Christian reader."

CHAPTER IV.

CONTINUED EFFORTS TO SUPPRESS THE ANTISLAVERY MOVEMENT BY FORCE AND INTIMIDATION.—FAVOURABLE EFFECT UPON THE PUBLIC MIND PRODUCED BY JAY'S WRITINGS.

THE second anniversary of the American Antislavery Society was held at the Presbyterian Church at Houston and Thompson Streets in New York on the 12th of May, 1835. James G. Birney, of Kentucky, George Thompson, of England, and William Lloyd Garrison made addresses. Judge Jay was appointed foreign corresponding secretary, and instructed to convey to the Duc de Broglie, president of the French Society for the Abolition of Slavery, the sympathy of American abolitionists.

The increasing activity and strength of the antislavery movement were not unnoticed by the partisans of the Slave Power, both North and South, and an incident occurred at Charleston, S. C., on the night of July 29th, which illustrated the temper and methods of the party. The American Antislavery Society had directed their publishers to forward a number of their periodical papers presenting facts and arguments on the subject of slavery to various Southern gentlemen of distinction in the hope of inspiring a spirit of inquiry among persons of influence and character. "But it was precisely this spirit of inquiry," said Judge Jay, "that the advocates of perpetual bondage feared might be fatal to their favourite institution. Hence they affected to believe that the papers sent to the masters were intended to incite the slaves to insurrection." The fact that a considerable number of antislavery publications had arrived at Charleston became known, and a mob broke into the post-office and burned the mail in the streets. Arthur Tappan, William L. Garrison, and Rev. Samuel H. Cox were burned in effigy. Mass meetings were held at Charleston and Richmond to approve the action of the mob, and aroused great excitement throughout the country. A committee was appointed at Charleston to take charge of the Northern mail on its arrival and to see that no antislavery papers should reach their destinations. The postmaster advised the postmaster-general that under existing circumstances he had determined to suppress all antislavery publications, and asked for instructions. Amos Kendall, Jackson's postmaster-general, whose sworn duty it was to preserve the sanctity of the mails, was only too willing to act as the tool of the Slave Power. "We owe," he replied, "an obligation to the laws, but a higher one to the communities in which we live, and if the former be perverted to destroy the latter, it is patriotism to disregard them. Entertaining these views, I *cannot sanction and will not condemn the step you have taken.*" These novel and dangerous doctrines, by which the laws of the republic were to be set aside by public officers for political purposes, received the sanction of President Jackson.

The postmaster at New York, Samuel L. Gouverneur, proposed to the American Antislavery Society that it voluntarily desist from sending its publications by mail, but the Executive Committee properly refused to yield the legal rights which they possessed in common with their fellow-citizens. The postmaster announced that antislavery papers would not be forwarded until further notice, and wrote to Washington for instructions. Kendall replied that he was "deterred from giving an order to exclude the whole series of antislavery publications from the Southern mail only by a want of legal power." Such a power, he admitted, vested in the head of the post-office department, would be fearfully dangerous and had been withheld properly; but he added, with more regard to the public opinion of the moment than to the principles of the Constitution, "If I were situated as you are, I would do as you have done." Some members of the Executive Committee wished to test the action of the New York postmaster in the United States courts, but Judge Jay opposed the plan for reasons which he gave in a letter to Elizur Wright, Jr.: "The action must be brought and tried in the city of New York—in that city in which this same gentleman, after his offence had been publicly proclaimed by himself in the newspapers, addressed thousands of the citizens in the Park and was received by their applause. Nor is this all. His conduct is commended by his superior, who is a member of the President's cabinet and probably acts with the approbation of General Jackson. Under such circumstances, I think it improbable that a prosecution would be attended with any result beneficial to our cause. We have not surrendered our rights, but they have been violently wrested from us. . . . *Festina lente* is sometimes a safe maxim. Fidelity to our principles and prudence in our conduct will, in time, through the blessing of God, crown our labours with success. You think it is hardly to be supposed that the people of the North are willing to give up the right of the post-office. Certainly they are not willing to give up their own, but they are willing *at present* to give up *our* right to it."

The South, recognizing the growing strength of antislavery opinion, began its appeals to the North to save the Union by suppressing the abolitionists. A public meeting in Virginia requested that this might be done "by strong yet lawful, by mild yet constitutional means"—terms which recalled the inquisitor of the Holy Office handing over condemned heretics to the executioner with the ironical request that he would deal with them tenderly and without blood-letting. In deference to the Slave Power the post-office had been made to nullify the freedom of the press, and freedom of speech was now to be suppressed, if possible, by mob violence. The situation of abolitionists in this year may be inferred from letters written from Brooklyn during the summer by Mrs. Lydia Maria Child: "I have not ventured into the city, nor does one of us dare to go to church to-day, so great is the excitement here. You can form no conception of it. 'Tis like the times of the French Revolution, when no man dared trust his neighbour. Private assassins from New Orleans are lurking at the corners of the streets to stab Arthur Tappan; and very large sums are offered for any one who will get Mr. George Thompson into the slave States. I tremble for him. He is almost a close prisoner in his chamber, his friends deeming him in eminent peril the moment it is ascertained where he is. . . . Five thousand dollars were offered on the Exchange in New York for the head of Arthur Tappan on Friday last. Elizur Wright is barricading his house with shutters, bars, and bolts. Judge Jay has been with us two or three days. He is as firm as the everlasting hills."

The popular feeling against the abolitionists was growing daily, and from every quarter they were charged with "unconstitutional, insurrectionary, and diabolical designs." To attempt to disabuse the community of the false impressions received from proslavery speakers and newspapers seemed the most important duty at this time. The following anonymous letter, signed "A Returning Southerner," was received by Arthur Tappan, and placed the necessity for such action in a strong light:

"Though we are unknown to each other, yet the friendship I feel for you induces me to address you. I have been where you have not, and have heard what you have not, and believe that great prudence is requisite on your part. I do not ask you to remit your philanthropic efforts. Heaven and and future ages, if not the present, will appreciate them.

"I do not pretend to advise, but have often thought that you and your friends do not take sufficient means to disabuse the public of the ceaseless charges of a multitude of papers.

"A vast majority in this city have never seen one of your papers, and countless multitudes, not only here but through our vast republic, believe without a doubt, for they have seen it unceasingly asserted and never contradicted, that you ardently wish your incendiary publications to excite the slaves to rebellion and bloodshed, massacre and rapine in their worst forms. While this impression is so common, or rather so universal, I was glad to see in circulation, as tending in some measure to your safety and the safety of this association, that you address not the slave but his master—a fact well enough known by your vengeance-seeking foes, but not known by those whom they intend to use as instruments of violence. I only presume further to suggest a card, to be inserted at least a week in the *Courier and Inquirer*, stating in brief terms that you do not advocate the violence imputed to you; that you address the reason of white men, not the passions of slaves."

The Executive Committee of the American Antislavery Society resolved to ask Judge Jay to prepare such a statement as the crisis called for. Jay was on a tour through the White Mountains at the time, but immediately on his return he prepared the following address, which was published in September, 1835, and was widely circulated in America and Europe:

"*To the Public.*

"In behalf of the American Antislavery Society we solicit the candid attention of the public to the following declaration of our principles and objects. Were the charges which are brought against us made only by persons who are interested in the continuance of slavery, and by such as are influenced solely by unworthy motives, this address would be unnecessary; but there are those who merit and possess our esteem, who would not voluntarily do us injustice, and who have been led by gross misrepresentations to believe that we are pursuing measures at variance not only with the constitutional rights of the South but with the precepts of humanity and religion. To such we offer the following explanations and assurances:

"1st. We hold that Congress has no more right to abolish slavery in the Southern States than in the French West India Islands. Of course we desire no national legislation on the subject.

"2d. We hold that slavery cannot be lawfully abolished except by the Legislatures of the several States in which it prevails, and that the exercise of any other than moral influence to induce such abolition is unconstitutional.

"3d. We believe that Congress has the same right to abolish

slavery in the District of Columbia that the State governments have within their respective jurisdictions, and that it is their duty to efface so foul a spot from the national escutcheon.

"4th. We believe the American citizens have the right to express and publish their opinions of the constitutions, laws, and institutions of any and every State and nation under heaven; and we mean never to surrender the liberty of speech, of the press, or of conscience—blessings we have inherited from our fathers, and which we intend, so far as we are able, to transmit unimpaired to our children.

"5th. We have uniformly deprecated all forcible attempts on the part of the slaves to recover their liberty; and were it in our power to address them we would exhort them to observe a quiet and peaceful demeanour, and would assure them that no insurrectionary movement on their part would receive from us the slightest aid or countenance.

"6th. We would deplore any servile insurrection, both on account of the calamities which would attend it and on account of the occasion which it would furnish of increased severity and oppression.

"7th. We are charged with sending incendiary publications to the South. If by the term 'incendiary' is meant publications containing arguments and facts to prove slavery to be a moral and political evil, and that duty and policy require its immediate abolition, the charge is true. But if this term is used to imply publications encouraging insurrection and designed to excite the slaves to break their fetters, the charge is utterly and unequivocally false. We beg our fellow-citizens to notice that this charge is made without proof, and by many who confess that they have never read our publications, and that those who make it offer to the public no evidence from our writings in support of it.

"8th. We are accused of sending our publications to the slaves, and it is asserted that their tendency is to excite insurrections. Both the charges are false. These publications are not intended for the slaves, and were they able to read them, they would find in them no encouragement to insurrection.

"9th. We are accused of employing agents in the slave States to distribute our publications. We have never had one such agent. We have sent no packages of our papers to any person in those States for distribution, except to five respectable resident citizens at their own request. But we have sent by mail single papers addressed to public officers, editors of newspapers, and clergymen. If, therefore, our object is to excite the slaves to insurrection, the masters are our agents!

"10th. We believe slavery to be sinful, injurious to this and to every other country in which it prevails; we believe immediate emancipation to be the duty of every slaveholder, and that the immediate abolition of slavery, by those who have the right to abolish it, would be safe and wise. These opinions we have freely expressed, and we certainly have no intention to refrain from expressing them in future, and urging them upon the consciences and hearts of our fellow-citizens who hold slaves or apologize for slavery.

"11th. We believe that the education of the poor is required by duty, and by a regard for the permanency of our republican institutions. There are thousands and tens of thousands of our fellow-citizens, even in the free States, sunk in abject poverty, and who, on account of their complexion, are virtually kept in ignorance, and whose instruction in certain cases is actually prohibited by law. We are anxious to protect the rights and to promote the virtue and happiness of the coloured portion of our population, and on this account we have been charged with a design to encourage intermarriage between the whites and the blacks. This charge has been repeatedly and is now again denied; while we repeat that the tendency of our sentiments is to put an end to the criminal amalgamation that prevails wherever slavery exists.

"12th. We are accused of acts that tend to a dissolution of the Union, and even of wishing to dissolve it. We have never 'calculated the value of the Union,' because we believe it to be inestimable, and that the abolition of slavery will remove the chief danger of its dissolution; and one of the many reasons why we endeavour to preserve the Constitution is that it restrains Congress from making any law 'abridging the freedom of speech or of the press.'

"Such, fellow-citizens, are our principles. Are they unworthy of Christians and of republicans? Or are they in truth so atrocious that in order to prevent their diffusion you are yourselves willing to surrender at the dictation of others the invaluable privilege of free discussion, the very birthright of Americans? Will you, in order that the abominations of slavery may be concealed from public view, and that the capital of your republic may continue to be as it now is, under the sanction of Congress, the great slave-mart of the American continent, consent that the general government, in acknowledged defiance of the Constitution and laws, shall appoint throughout the length and breadth of your land ten thousand censors of the press, each of whom shall have the right to inspect every document you may commit to the post-office, and to suppress every pamphlet and newspaper, whether religious or political, which in his sovereign pleasure he may adjudge to contain an incendiary article? Surely we need not remind you that if you submit to such an encroachment on your liberties the days of our republic are numbered, and that although abolitionists may be the first, they will not be the last victims offered at the shrine of arbitrary power.

"(Signed)
"ARTHUR TAPPAN,
"JOHN RANKIN,
"WILLIAM JAY,
"ELIZUR WRIGHT, Jr.,
"ABRAHAM L. COX,
"LEWIS TAPPAN,
"JOSHUA LEAVITT,
"SAMUEL E. CORNISH,
"SIMEON S. JOCELIN,
"THEODORE S. WRIGHT.

"NEW YORK, September 3d, 1835."

The effect of Jay's address to the public was thus described by Elizur Wright, Jr.: "The Southern papers are copying it extensively, and most of them charge us with having disclaimed in it our real motives—a proof that our real sentiments were before misunderstood. In a large number of Northern papers it is copied with more or less approbation. Indeed, none but the determined pro-slavery presses fail to speak of it as a candid, firm, and honourable if not convincing document." "It has had a most beneficial effect," wrote Lewis Tappan. "What a contrast to the ebullition of public meetings!"

A movement was begun in the year 1835, on the part of the Southern press and Southern Legislatures to induce penal legislation in the North against the expression of antislavery sentiments. The *Richmond Whig* revealed its opinion of its Northern allies when it said: "Depend upon it, the Northern people will never sacrifice their lucrative trade with the South so long as the hanging of a few thousands will prevent it." In obedience to these demands, pro-slavery men in the North were actually to be found proposing legislation intended to destroy the freedom of the press and to make antislavery expression a criminal offence. Judge Jay took occasion to meet this movement in a charge which he delivered to the Westchester Grand Jury, in which he said: "Any law which might be passed to abridge in the slightest degree the freedom of speech or of the press, or to shield any one subject from discussion, would be utterly null and void; and it would be the duty of every genuine republican to resist with energy and decision so palpable an outrage on the declared will of the people." These remarks were widely published and did much to discourage the pro-slavery agitators.

But other illegitimate and violent schemes to reduce to silence antislavery men were soon brought into play. South Carolina having inaugurated the assault upon the constitutional rights of the North through the post-office, Alabama followed in a yet bolder step against the personal security of abolitionists. Governor Gayle, of that State, demanded of the Governor of New York that Ransom G. Williams, the publishing agent of the Antislavery Society, should be surrendered to him to be tried under the laws of Alabama on an indictment found against him by the Grand Jury for publishing in the *Emancipator*, in the city of New York, the following sentiment: "God commands and all nature cries out that man should not be held as property. The system of making men property has plunged two and a quarter millions of our fellow-countrymen into the deepest physical and moral degradation, and they are every moment sinking deeper." This expression was the most offensive which the Alabama Grand Jury could discover in the documents of the society on which to base the indictment and demand, and as the one which came nearest to anything resembling an attempt to incite the slaves to insurrection. Williams had never been in the State of Alabama, was never subject to its laws, had never fled from its jurisdiction, and these facts were admitted by the Governor when he made requisition for Williams as a "fugitive from justice." While the American Antislavery Society was considering what action it should take for the protection of its agent, Lewis Tappan wrote to Judge Jay (8th September) suggesting that he should get the opinion of two or three eminent lawyers on the subject to be circulated by the society. Jay replied: "The Southern papers have intimated that Northern abolitionists may be indicted in the courts and then demanded of the State executives, and you request my opinion whether it would be advisable to obtain and publish the legal opinion of eminent counsel on this novel doctrine. The doctrine is so monstrous, so utterly at variance with all our ideas of constitutional and State rights, that it shocks the understanding and moral sense of the community, and I verily believe that there is not one Northern governor who would dare to arrest a citizen on such a demand. But if we manifest alarm at this doctrine and get lawyers to controvert it, there will be found rival presses, venal lawyers, and corrupt politicians to support the other side of the question; the community will begin to discuss the subject, passion and interest and prejudice will believe whatever they want to believe. My opinion, therefore, is that the less we say on this subject the better, and that we should not give a factitious importance to the doctrine." Jay's advice was followed and proved to be wise. Governor Marcy could do nothing but refuse the request of Governor Gayle, although he softened his refusal by abuse of the abolitionists.

Under the leadership of Alvan Stewart a convention was called to meet at Utica on October 21, 1835, to form a New York State Antislavery Society. About six hundred delegates were present. The spirit of mob violence, which was being encouraged by pro-slavery orators and presses throughout the country to suppress the abolitionists by force, was relied upon to prevent the meeting of the convention. The mob having occupied in advance the room in the court-house prepared for the meeting, the delegates repaired to a Presbyterian Church, where they had barely enough time to organize and elect officers before the riotous supporters of slavery broke into the church and violently dispersed the convention. The lawless tyranny to which the delegates were subjected and their courageous conduct attracted to their cause many persons who had held aloof hitherto. Chief among these was Gerrit Smith, who from this time gave to the antislavery movement unstinted contributions of money and intelligent labour. Judge Jay, notwithstanding his unavoidable absence from the convention, was elected president of the society then formed.

At about the same time as the Utica riots occurred the mobbing of William Lloyd Garrison, in Boston, by "gentlemen of property and standing." And all over the North were enacted scenes of violence, encouraged by a large portion of the press, which were intended to gratify the Southern demand that abolitionism should be put down at all hazards. The sanctity of the mails, the constitutional right of free speech and of lawful assemblage, were forgotten by a large portion of the people. And they were forgotten by the President of the United States himself. In December, 1835, Andrew Jackson, in his message to Congress, gave a tacit approval to mob rule, to the suppression of the freedom of the press, and to the oft-exposed falsehood that the abolitionists distributed documents among the slaves intended to incite them to insurrection; and he recommended the closing of the mails to antislavery people.

The position taken by President Jackson was so unjust, so unconstitutional, and so calculated to aggravate the situation, that the American Anti-slavery Society determined to make an official reply to it. Judge Jay was chosen to answer the President on behalf of the society, and he prepared an address which was signed by all the officers. This document was a complete exposure of the falsity of the charges made and of the unlawfulness of the restrictive measures which Jackson proposed to Congress.

"You have accused," said Jay, "an indefinite number of your fellow-citizens, without designation of name or residence, of making unconstitutional and wicked efforts, and of harbouring intentions which could be entertained only by the most depraved and abandoned of mankind; and yet you carefully abstain from averring *which* article of the Constitution they have transgressed; you omit stating when, where, and by whom these wicked attempts were made; you give no specification of the inflammatory appeals which you assert have been addressed to the passions of the slaves. You well know that the 'moral influence' of your charges will affect thousands and tens of thousands of your countrymen, many of them your political friends—some of them heretofore honoured with your confidence—most, if not all of them, of irreproachable character; and yet, by the very vagueness of your charges, you incapacitate each one of this multitude from proving his innocence. . . . It is deserving of notice that the *attempt* to circulate our papers is alone charged upon us. It is not pretended that we have put our appeals into the hands of a single slave, or that in any instance our endeavours to excite a servile war have been crowned with success. And in what way was our most execrable attempt made? By secret agents, traversing the slave country in disguise, stealing by night into the hut of the slave, and reading to him our inflammatory appeals? You, sir, answer this question by declaring that we attempted the mighty mischief by circulating our appeals *through the mails!* And are the Southern slaves, sir, accustomed to receive periodicals by mail? Of the thousands of publications mailed from the antislavery office for the South, did you ever hear, sir, of one solitary paper being addressed to a slave? Would you know to whom they were directed, consult the Southern newspapers, and you will find them complaining that they were sent to public officers, clergymen, and other influential citizens. Thus, it seems, we are incendiaries who place the torch in the hands of him whose dwelling we would fire! We are conspiring to incite a servile war, and announce our design to the masters and commit to their care and disposal the very instruments by which we expect to effect our purpose! . . . To repel your charges and to disabuse the public was a duty we owed to ourselves, to our children, and, above all, to the great and holy cause in which we are engaged. That cause we believe is approved by our Maker; and while we retain this belief, it is our intention, trusting to His direction and protection, to persevere in our endeavours to impress upon the minds and hearts of our countrymen the sinfulness of claiming property in human beings, and the duty and wisdom of immediately relinquishing it. When convinced that our endeavours are wrong, we shall abandon them, but such conviction must be produced by other arguments than vituperation, popular violence, or penal enactments."

In 1836 Judge Jay resigned the presidency of the New York State Antislavery Society. The distance of his home from the headquarters of the society made the office nearly nominal, and he thought that it should be filled by a person more favourably situated for usefulness. "We commenced the present struggle," he wrote in his letter of resignation, "to obtain the freedom of the slave; we are compelled to continue it to preserve our own. We are now contending, not so much with the slaveholders of the South about human rights, as with the political and commercial aristocracy of the North, for the liberty of speech, of the press, and of conscience. Our politicians are selling our constitutions and laws for Southern votes. Our great capitalists are speculating, not merely in land and banks, but in the liberties of the people. We are called to contemplate a spectacle never, I believe, before witnessed—the wealthy portion of the community striving to introduce anarchy and violence on a calculation of profit; making merchandise of peace and good order! In Boston we have seen the editor of a newspaper led through the streets with a halter by gentlemen 'of property and standing.' The New York mobs were excited, not by the humble penny press, but by the malignant falsehood and insurrectionary appeals of certain commercial journals. Rich and honourable men in Cincinnati have recently at a public meeting proclaimed lynch law, and through their influence a printing-press devoted to freedom has been destroyed,

and the whole affair, we are coolly and most truly told, was a *business transaction.*

"... It cannot be, it is not in human nature that judges and lawyers and rich merchants will long enjoy the exclusive privileges of trampling on the laws. These men are sowing the wind and they will reap the whirlwind. They may see the buddings of their harvest in the recent assaults upon the Holland Land Company. When the tempest of anarchy they are now raising shall sweep over the land it will not be the humble abolitionist, but the lofty possessor of power and fortune, who will first be levelled by the blast. . . . The obligations of religion and of patriotism; the duties we owe to ourselves, to our children, the cause of freedom, and the cause of humanity—all require us to be faithful to our principles, to persevere in our exertions, and to surrender our rights only with our breath. Duties are ours and consequences are God's, and while we discharge the first we may be confident that the latter will be entirely consistent with our true welfare."

CHAPTER V.

GRADUAL DECLINE OF RIOTOUS DEMONSTRATIONS AGAINST THE ABOLITIONISTS.—CHANGES OCCUR IN THE DOCTRINES AND METHODS OF THE AMERICAN ANTISLAVERY SOCIETY.—JUDGE JAY RESIGNS HIS MEMBERSHIP, WHILE CONTINUING HIS EFFORTS ON BEHALF OF EMANCIPATION.

THE effort to suppress the antislavery movement by force, which was carried on by Northern people at the instigation of the South, continued through the years 1837 and 1838. The incidents which attracted the most attention were the murder of Lovejoy at Alton and the burning of Pennsylvania Hall in Philadelphia by a mob. By assassination and arson a considerable portion of the American people sought to destroy the right to free speech and free assemblage guaranteed by the American Constitution and cherished hitherto as a birthright. The right of free discussion, wrote Alexander H. Everett at the time, "is not only endangered, but for the present, at least, is actually lost." "The newspapers of every day," he continued, "bring to our view the account of some new case in which a printing-press has been seized and thrown into the river; a public meeting broken up; a citizen tarred and feathered, scourged—too often, I add with horror, put to a violent death by a lawless mob for no other cause or crime than the free discussion of the subject of slavery." The impunity with which these crimes were committed, the connivance or leniency of the authorities whose sworn duty it was to uphold the laws, made this time a critical one for the security of American liberties. In pursuing their lawful course undaunted through this "reign of terror," when so large a portion of their fellow-countrymen seemed to have forgotten the obligations of citizens to established law, the abolitionists not only maintained the existence of their cause, but they preserved those rights which Americans value above all others. That free speech continued to exist in the United States was due to their indomitable courage. Such a state of affairs could not endure long. Lawless feeling exhausted itself in fruitless violence. Antislavery societies increased in numbers and membership. Comparative order and toleration gradually displaced the disgraceful passions which had placed the liberties of the country in hazard.

As opposition diminished and their path became easier, abolitionists began to differ among themselves as to the best means to attain their ends and as to the fundamental principles of their cause. In New York State a tendency was developed, under the leadership of Gerrit Smith, to adopt political methods. In Boston moral agitation remained the accepted means. But here novel theories on other subjects were being adopted by leading antislavery people and thus associated in the public mind with antislavery itself. Garrison adopted and recommended in the *Liberator* his no-government and non-résistance doctrines. He put forth new and not generally accepted views regarding the observance of Sunday. He took pains to declare that he adopted these theories in his private capacity, and not as an abolitionist. But he had many followers who did not discriminate so carefully. The public mind became confused and began to associate abolitionism with a variety of novel and unpopular opinions. The cause was thus obstructed and divisions occurred among those who laboured for the emancipation of the negro. Up to this time women had not taken part in public meetings, and to many persons the idea of their doing so was repugnant. The admission of women to membership and office in the same societies as men was determined in Boston in 1838, after a struggle and amidst much objection.

"I have observed," wrote Jay in a private letter in 1838, "frequent attempts to use abolition as a packhorse to carry forth into the world some favourite notion having no legitimate connection with the antislavery cause; and have witnessed the dissensions caused in our ranks by such inconsiderate and dishonest assumptions. Thus I have known an official document, under the signature of a secretary of a State society, pass a high eulogium on a particular form of Church government; and I have seen an editorial article in an official antislavery periodical recommending a decoction of dried currants as a substitute for the fermented juice of the grape in the observance of the Lord's Supper! All such perversions of antislavery influence appear to me to be dishonest in their character, and dangerous in their consequences to the continuance and efficiency of our organization. No one is more strenuous than myself for the right of opinion and discussion; but common justice and fairness require that we should not make others responsible for our peculiar opinions, nor seek to propagate them by means entrusted to us for very different purposes.

"The practice of passing numerous resolutions at our antislavery meetings strikes me as a growing and pernicious evil. Too many seem to think that all our objects are to be effected by resolutions; and amid the vast multitude that are proposed and adopted with little reflection, it is not surprising, yet deeply to be deplored, that some are false *in fact*, more false in sentiment, and very many coarse and vulgar in expression. Falsehood is not the less immoral for being employed in a good cause, and it is very unwise to impair the charms of Truth by arraying her in vulgar attire. It is to be wished that our meetings may in future be less prodigal of their resolutions, and more circumspect as to the matter and language."

Judge Jay looked with dismay upon the novel doctrines on other subjects which were becoming associated with antislavery in the public mind. He deplored the loss of strength which must result from a departure from the singleness of purpose announced in the declaration of principles at the founding of the American Antislavery Society. And there were differences of opinion arising on the fundamental principles of the cause which troubled him still more. As has been shown in these pages, he had joined the American Antislavery Society only after a deliberate examination of its constitution and the conviction that its principles were in strict accordance with the Constitution of the United States. He was as strong an advocate of emancipation as lived, but to him the Constitution was the supreme law under which all benefits could be and must be obtained. Efforts to seek the abolition of slavery by arguments or conduct in violation of the Constitution seemed to him wicked in themselves and fatal to the cause. Such efforts he had now to combat.

At the sixth anniversary of the Massachusetts Antislavery Society, held in January, 1838, the business committee, composed of Messrs. Garrison, Phelps, May, and Fairbanks, reported the following resolution:

"*Resolved,* That in order to bring our coloured friends within the brotherhood of this nation, we will encourage them in petitioning to Congress, in their own names, for the redress of their grievances, and, if not successful, then we will lend them our aid in bringing their cause before the court of the United States to ascertain if a man can be held in bondage agreeably to the principles contained in the Declaration of Independence or the Constitution of our country."

Judge Jay wrote a letter to Mr. Ellis Gray Loring, March 5th, asking for more definite information as to the true intent of the society in passing the resolution.

"Who are the *coloured friends* alluded to?" he asked. "Obviously *slaves*, because if Congress does not redress their grievances, then the society is to lead them into the court of the United States to ascertain whether a man can be held in *bondage*.

"What grievances are the slaves, under the encouragement of the society, to petition Congress to redress? Obviously those they suffer as slaves, because if Congress does not redress them, redress is to be sought in the court, by demanding if a man can be held in *bondage*, that is, as a slave.

"What slaves are intended by the resolution? No qualification or limitation whatever is expressed or implied. The Society, no doubt, recognizes the slaves of Georgia as its coloured friends as well as the slaves of the District of Columbia. The resolution is the tenth of a series of resolutions reported by the committee, and in none of them is any mention made of the District of Columbia, and, moreover, the question to be decided by the court is not whether an inhabitant of the District can be held as a slave, but whether a man can be held in bondage agreeably to the principles of the Declaration of Independence and the Constitution of our country, and the tribunal to decide this question is not the court of the District but the court of the United States.

"Members of Congress take an oath to support the Constitution of the United States. If, therefore, the society believe the Constitution does not authorize Congress to redress the grievances of its coloured friends, it has pledged itself to encourage those friends to petition Congress to commit perjury. Hence it appears to me that the true meaning of this resolution, expressed in plain language, is, ' *Resolved,* That in our opinion Congress possesses the constitutional power to abolish slavery throughout the United States, and that we will encourage the slaves to petition Congress for an act of emancipation, and should no such an act be passed we will aid them in suing for their freedom in the Supreme Court of the United States.'

"It is to be regretted that the society did not announce the means they intend to employ to encourage the slaves to send petitions to Congress. The pledge has been solemnly given. Is it to be redeemed by sending among them secret or avowed agents? It is singular also that if the society believes the ' court of the United States ' can give liberty to the slaves, it should not make an *immediate* application for its beneficent interposition, but should resolve to postpone such application not only until it has succeeded in prompting them to petition Congress for a redress of their grievances, but also until a sufficient time has elapsed to learn the result of this moral experiment. Permit me now, sir, to call your attention to the past professions of some of the gentlemen who reported this resolution, and of the society which adopted it.

"On the 4th December, 1833, Messrs. Phelps, Garrison, and May, as members of the Philadelphia Convention, signed the following declaration: ' We fully and unanimously recognize the sovereignty of *each State to legislate exclusively* on the subject of slavery which is tolerated within its limits. We concede that Congress has no *right to interfere* with any slave State in relation to the momentous subject.'

"Mr. Garrison afterwards, in an editorial article in the *Liberator*, thus expresses himself: 'Abolitionists as clearly understand and as sacredly regard the constitutional powers of Congress as do their traducers, and they know, and have again and again asserted, that Congress has *no more rightful authority to sit in judgment upon Southern slavery than it has to legislate for the abolition of slavery in the French colonies.*'

"On the 17th of August, 1835, at a meeting of the Massachusetts Antislavery Society, duly held in Boston, an address to the public was adopted, professing to set forth the *true principles and objects* of the society; and to give this statement a stronger claim to the confidence of the community it was authenticated by the signatures of *thirty-one* of the principal officers and members of the society, including *your own* and those of three of the committee who reported the late resolution, viz., Messrs. Garrison, May, and Fairbanks. The opinion of the society at that time on the power of Congress was in that document thus explicitly stated: 'We fully acknowledge that no change in the slave laws of the Southern States can be made unless by the Southern Legislatures. Neither Congress nor the Legislatures of the free States have authority *to change the condition* of a single slave in the slave States.' Yet the society now stands prepared to encourage the slaves to petition Congress for a redress of their grievances! And now, sir, the object of this letter is to ascertain whether the resolution I have quoted does in truth represent the present opinion held by your society on the power of Congress, or whether the resolution was intended to be confined to slaves in the District of Columbia and the territory of Florida.

"It cannot be necessary to dwell on the vast importance of an explicit declaration by your board on this subject. Independent of the deep concern I feel in the harmony, integrity, and consistency of the abolition party, I have a personal interest in the inquiry I now make of you. An *enlarged* edition of my book is ready for the press, but the late resolution of your society compels me to suspend its publication. I had treated the charge that abolitionists desired Congress to interfere with slavery in the States as calumnious, and in refutation of it had appealed to their solemn disclaimers. I need not say, sir, that until the late resolution is satisfactorily explained, or its doctrine disavowed by your society, I cannot in my new edition deny the charge, but must as an honest man substitute for my confident assertions and triumphant appeals most painful and humiliating confessions. Permit me to suggest that it is highly desirable that your board should act explicitly on this subject before the meeting of the American Antislavery Society, that, if possible, no inquiries or investigation may then arise to mar the harmony of the meeting and retard the progress of abolition.

"I flatter myself, sir, that your sentiments on the constitutional question remain the same as when you signed the address of 1835, and that you comprehend and appreciate the motives which have prompted this letter. I shall await your answer with extreme anxiety."

On receipt of this letter Mr. Loring communicated with a number of the members of the board of managers and endeavoured to hold a meeting of the board for the purpose of rescinding or repudiating the resolution; but it was not until the 14th that he succeeded in getting a quorum together. After Mr. Loring had read Judge Jay's letter to the board, they promptly passed the following resolution:

"*Resolved*, That as said resolution was submitted to the meeting just at its close, when but few delegates were present, and was adopted without deliberation or discussion, this board recommend its reconsideration at the next quarterly meeting of the society.

"*Resolved*, As the sense of this board, that Congress has no power to abolish slavery in the several States of this Union."

In a letter dated the 15th of March, enclosing a copy of the above resolution, Mr. Loring said: "I can hear of but one or two persons here who believe in the power of Congress over slavery in the States, viz., the Misses Grimke, Mr. Alanson St. Clair, and perhaps Mr. May and Mrs. Chapman. Several, however, and those influential persons (Mr. Garrison among them), think slavery unconstitutional, and believe it would be so pronounced by the Supreme Court of the United States if the point should ever be made. In this opinion I can by no means agree."

The "unfortunate resolution," he continued, was offered by a "silly officious person" at a moment of much haste and confusion just as the meeting was breaking up, and had been approved without proper consideration by the committee whose duty it was to revise all resolutions. "It seems, however, to have been understood by those who voted for it as applying only to free coloured persons whose rights might be infringed by Southern laws or to slaves in the District of Columbia; and the pledge given to try the question of slavery in the United States Courts seems to have arisen from the notion that the question of the accordance of slavery with the Constitution might be incidentally raised and determined even in a case in which the party whose rights are to be vindicated is free."

In conclusion Mr. Loring said that this question would assume an important aspect at the future meetings of the Antislavery Society, and earnestly hoped wise and honest counsel would prevail. He thought it would be sufficient ground for dissolving the Union were the United States Supreme Court to assume power over slavery in the several States. "The honesty and common sense of the nation," he wrote, "would revolt against such a doctrine and against those who should maintain it."

In his reply, dated the 29th of March, Judge Jay congratulated Mr. Loring on the service he had rendered the cause of abolition by procuring the passage of the resolutions from the board of managers. "In the fulness of our zeal," he wrote, "we are all liable occasionally to stray beyond the line of propriety, and it evinces more devotion to duty to acknowledge and correct errors than to avoid committing them."

At the fifth annual meeting of the American Antislavery Society, held at the Broadway Tabernacle on the 2d of May, 1838, Alvan Stewart of Utica, N. Y., offered a resolution, vigorously supported by himself and others, to the following effect:

"That the clause of the second article of the constitution of this society be struck out which admits 'that each State in which slavery exists has, by the Constitution of the United States, the exclusive right to legislate in regard to its abolition in said State.'"

This motion was equivalent to a declaration on the part of the society that Congress had the right, under the Constitution, to abolish slavery. Judge Jay had previously declared that Stewart's doctrine was false, untenable, and hurtful to the cause. The arguments by which it was supported he considered absurd. For two days of continued debate he exposed its fallacy and danger and was rewarded by the defeat of the resolution. But such attempts to change the original articles of belief upon which the society was founded gave him great uneasiness for the future. His feelings upon this subject were shown in a letter to the secretary of the Young Men's Antislavery Society who had invited him to preside at its convention:

"On uniting with the American Antislavery Society some years since I remarked, with the letter requesting that my name might be enrolled among its members, that I had attentively considered its constitution, and expressed my conviction that in joining the society I was acting consistently with my obligations as a Christian and a citizen. The great moral principles advanced in the constitution perfectly accorded, in my opinion, with the precepts of the Gospel, and the measures proposed, by which those principles were to be carried into practice, equally accorded with the obligations of the oath

I had taken to support the Constitution of the United States. I embarked in the antislavery cause with a firm determination to support the principles and measures avowed by the society at the hazard of obloquy, persecution, and, if necessary, even life itself; and never in advocating the cause to sacrifice truth and principle to expediency. How far I have acted up to this determination others must judge. I am not myself conscious of having departed from it.

"The constitution of the society contains an express admission that 'each State in which slavery exists has, by the Constitution of the United States, the exclusive right to legislate in regard to its abolition;' and the object of the society in regard to slavery in the States is declared to be to effect its abolition by 'arguments addressed to the understandings and consciences of our fellow-citizens.' Notwithstanding these explicit declarations we were accused of aiming to effect our object by inducing Congress to invade the rights of the States by abolishing slavery within their limits; and it was justly argued that such an attempt was unconstitutional, and would, if successful, lead to civil war and a severance of the Union. So gross and unfounded were the calumnies circulated against us, that it was deemed expedient by the executive committee of the society, of which I was one, to publish an address to the public, pledging our individual characters and responsibility as to the real objects and principles entertained by our association. This address bore my signature among others, and contained, as nearly as I can recollect, the following passage: 'We hold that Congress has no more right to abolish slavery in the States in which it exists than it has to abolish slavery in the French West India Islands; consequently we desire no national legislation on the subject.' We were justified in giving this pledge by the declaration of the convention which formed the society, by the constitution of the society itself, by the constitutions of the several State societies, and by the uniform language of antislavery publications. Few persons have been more conversant with the writings of abolitionists than myself; yet I can truly aver that until the appearance of Mr. Stewart's extraordinary argument I was not aware that there was a man or woman belonging to an antislavery society who entertained a different opinion. This gentleman, holding the responsible station of chairman of the executive committee of the State society, avowing in its constitution the inability of Congress to abolish slavery in the States, published an article in the official paper of the society, asserting the constitutional power of Congress immediately to emancipate every slave in the United States, declaring that abolitionists had 'but one thing to do'—which was to petition Congress to exercise this power; thus repudiating the moral means they had prescribed for themselves, viz., 'arguments addressed to the understandings and consciences of our fellow-citizens'; and virtually recommending the employment of *force*, the power of the general government as the sole agent in effecting the abolition of slavery.

"I had supposed that sentiments so utterly at variance with the solemn asseverations of abolitionists, so repugnant to the constitutional pledges of their societies, would have excited universal indignation; but I was mistaken. After the publication of these sentiments, Mr. Stewart was selected as one of the orators of the American Society at their ensuing anniversary. At the annual meeting in May last he moved to purge from the constitution the concession I have quoted, thus giving the society the constitutional right of discharging what he had proclaimed the sole duty of abolitionists, that of petitioning Congress to abolish slavery in the States; and in supporting his motion he ridiculed the idea of effecting our object by addresses to the understanding and consciences of slaveholders. On taking the question a majority of the society was in favour of expunging; and the admission respecting the power of Congress still stands in the constitution only because it required a vote of two thirds to cancel it. Mr. Stewart was afterwards elected a manager of the society. A State society since organized has by a formal vote refused to insert the usual admission into its constitution, and another previously organized has since stricken it from its constitution.

"From this state of facts it is apparent that the pledges given to the public in our constitution, and in the address of the executive committee to which I have referred, that abolitionists admitted that Congress had no right to interfere with slavery in the States, that hence arguments were the only means they intended to use for its abolition, have been flagrantly falsified. So far as I was concerned, and unquestionably many more, the pledge was given in good faith, and however others may belie it, I mean honestly to abide by it. In my opinion, Congress has no more right to pass a general emancipation law than to direct how Broadway shall be paved; and without intending to impeach the motives of others, I must take the liberty to say that I would regard such a law as a most wicked and detestable act of usurpation— an act that would inevitably and properly sever the Union and necessarily result in bloodshed and national calamity.

"It seems to me, moreover, inconsistent with Christian sincerity and plain dealing for our societies to profess in their constitution a belief in great and important principles, and to promise to regulate their measures in accordance with those principles, and at the same time to retain in communion with them and elevate to office men who openly repudiate and ridicule those principles and avow a wish to introduce a course of action utterly repugnant.

"On discovering from the proceedings of last May that the American Society and its auxiliaries no longer considered their avowed principles binding on their members, but that they might be treated with insult and ridicule without incurring a loss of either confidence or office, and that in the bosom of the society opinions were entertained utterly at variance with public and solemn professions, and in their practical consequences hostile to the welfare of the country and inconsistent with the oath I had taken to support the Constitution of the United States, I deemed it my duty no longer to share in the responsibilities of their measures. I have not since taken part in the meeting of any antislavery society, and the recklessness with which the pledge given by myself and other officers of the society has been falsified, warns me to be cautious how I again become identified with the promises and declarations of these associations. These considerations induce me very respectfully to decline your kind invitation.

"My attachment to the cause of abolition, and to the principles avowed in the constitution of the American Society, was never stronger than at this moment; and I shall ever regard it a duty and a privilege to labour for the abolition of slavery in every manner consistent with propriety and my moral and political obligations.

"Although my confidence in the integrity and singleness of purpose of antislavery societies is weakened, I have not the most distant wish to interrupt their harmony or impede their usefulness. I have thus, sir, frankly but with much pain stated my sentiments. These sentiments I have no desire to conceal or to obtrude upon others; and you are at liberty to suppress this letter or make any use of it you may think proper."

The annual meeting of the Connecticut Antislavery Society was held at New Haven in May, 1840, commencing on the 20th. The society considered this meeting to be of vital importance to the prosperity of the cause in that State on account of the Legislature being in session there at that time, many of the members of which were expected to attend.

In April Judge Jay received an invitation from the Committee of Arrangements to deliver an address on the "Action of the Federal Government in Behalf of Slavery," on which subject the Committee felt convinced that Judge Jay could "give the society as well as our legislators some valuable information."

Other engagements compelled Judge Jay to decline the invitation. In his letter to the Committee of Arrangements informing them of his inability to comply with their request, Judge Jay assured them that the interest he had theretofore professed to feel in the antislavery cause had suffered no diminution; and his conviction of the truth of the great principles set forth in the constitution of the American Society had, if possible, grown stronger from continued reflection and observation; but as to the singleness of purpose and the efficiency and integrity of the present antislavery organization his opinion had undergone a change.

"In joining the organization," he wrote, "I had good cause to believe that I would not be called upon to co-operate with men who condemned any of its avowed principles, or with men who would seek to render it an instrument for promoting other objects than the abolition of slavery.

"One of the principles laid down in the constitution of

the American Society, and a most important one as limiting its operations, is that by the Constitution of the United States Congress has no right to legislate for the abolition of slavery in the several States in which it exists. Yet a gentleman was in 1838 chosen by the society one of its officers after having both in print and in the presence of the society denied this doctrine and contended that it was the duty of abolitionists to petition Congress to pass a law for the immediate emancipation of all the slaves in the United States. The expulsion of this gentleman from the society was in my opinion required by the respect it owed itself, and by the good faith it owed both to the public and to its members. The course pursued was an emphatic declaration on the part of the society that its professed principles, however useful they might be in conciliating public confidence and in acquiring funds, were by no means binding on its members. Having sworn to support the Constitution of the United States, and regarding the proposed mode of emancipation a most palpable violation of it, and seeing that the avowed principles of the society were in fact no security for its conformity to them in its conduct, I then determined never again to take a part in its meetings or in those of its auxiliaries. Subsequent events have given me no cause to regret this determination.

"One of the great objects for which the American Society was avowedly formed was to effect the abolition of slavery in the District of Columbia and of the American slave-trade by Congressional legislation. Yet men belonging to the society, and even some of its officers, are now publicly maintaining that all compulsory laws are sinful, and of course that it would be a usurpation of the divine prerogative for Congress to suppress by penal law the abomination of slavery in the capital of the republic, and the nefarious traffic in human flesh of which the capital is the great depot. I cannot as an abolitionist act with those who reprobate all enactments, not merely for the abolition of slavery where it exists, but even for preventing its re-establishment on soil from which it has been extirpated; and also for protecting the poor coloured man, his wife, and children from the merciless kidnapper.

"Certainly the founders of the society did not intend to effect by it any alteration in the social relations of the sexes; and not the most distant hint of such a design can be found in the Constitution; yet it is in vain to deny that an attempt is now making to render antislavery societies instrumental in advancing certain theories respecting the rights of women.

"The American Society was intended as a central organization by which the contributions and efforts of abolitionists were to be concentrated and directed; and for some years it discharged its functions with wonderful zeal, energy, and success. But at last the managers of certain local societies imagined that the vitality of the extremities of the system would be quickened by arresting the pulsations of the heart; and accordingly measures were adopted, and with perfect success, to paralyze the parent institution.

"For a while abolitionists exhibited a pattern of Christian and disinterested benevolence in behalf of the oppressed which commanded the secret admiration even of their enemies, and conciliated the favour of the good. Latterly a strong desire has been evinced to change the antislavery enterprise from a religious into a political one, and a scramble for the loaves and fishes has already commenced.

"Unwilling to take a part in the bitter feuds which now divide abolitionists, and not choosing to assume any responsibility for principles and measures I cannot approve, I deem it most consistent with my obligations as a Christian and a citizen to absent myself from an arena in which I can do no good and in which I can no longer appear without being engaged in unprofitable conflict. But most cheerfully will I again enlist in a new antislavery organization (if any such can be devised) that will offer a fair promise of avoiding the errors which have destroyed the efficiency and moral character of the present.

"I beg you to be assured that in the preceding remarks I have had no particular reference to the Connecticut Society, not being aware that it is open to censure.

"I have no desire either to conceal or to obtrude my opinions respecting the existing state of the antislavery enterprise, but I deemed it due to myself to state frankly and without reserve the considerations which induce me to pursue a course apparently at variance with my former public vindication of the American Antislavery Society."

Among abolitionists there was a great diversity of opinion as to whether women should be admitted to membership in antislavery societies and permitted to hold office and generally to enjoy the same privileges as men. This question was the cause of much feeling and was destined to create an unfortunate division in the antislavery ranks.

The subject was first voted upon in the New England Society, where, in 1838, it was resolved to permit all persons, whether men or women, who agreed with them on the subject of slavery to participate in the meetings as members. An attempt having been made in vain to rescind this vote, a protest was drawn up by Amos R. Phelps, Charles T. Torrey, and five others, disclaiming all responsibility for it, and denouncing the action of the society as injurious to the cause of the slave by connecting with it an entirely foreign subject and by establishing a dangerous precedent.

At the sixth annual meeting of the American Anti-slavery Society, held in New York, May 7, 1839, it was voted, 180 ayes to 140 nays, "that the roll of the convention be made up by placing upon it the names of all persons, male or female, who are delegated from any auxiliary society, or members of this society."

The seventh annual meeting of the American Society was fixed for the 12th of May, 1840. It was generally realized that on this occasion a definitive settlement of the woman question would be made. The board of managers of the Massachusetts Society made strenuous efforts to insure a large attendance of members sharing their views. A large steamboat was chartered which conveyed Garrison and his party to New York, and it was soon manifest that they had mustered a majority sufficient to carry their point.

Arthur Tappan, the president of the society, anticipating "a recurrence of the scenes witnessed last year, and resolved not to be found contending with his abolition brethren," did not attend the meeting, and Francis Jackson presided in his place. Among the persons nominated by the chairman as a business committee was Miss Abby Kelley. After a long and exciting debate Miss Kelley was elected by a vote of 557 to 451. Immediately after the result was announced, Lewis Tappan, Charles W. Denison, and Amos Phelps, members of the business committee, asked to be excused from serving upon it.

After the meeting had adjourned those members who had voted against the admission of women met and organized a new society under the name of the "American and Foreign Antislavery Society." Arthur Tappan was chosen president, James G. Birney and Henry B. Stanton, secretaries, and Lewis Tappan, treasurer. The Executive Committee was composed of Gerrit Smith, Judge Jay, John G. Whittier, Joshua Leavitt, and other leading abolitionists.

On June 1st Judge Jay wrote a note to Mr. J. C. Jackson, the recording secretary of the American Antislavery Society, asking that his name be stricken from the roll as a member. In stating his reasons for resigning, he said that the proceedings at the late meeting of the society had convinced him that the institution was being used, by those who had recently acquired control of it, as an instrument for advancing the doctrine of the equality of the sexes in all the relations of life. "Married women without their husbands," he said, "were associated with men in the Executive Committee—a committee to which is confided the management of the society, and whose meetings have hitherto been, and will probably continue to be, both frequent and private."

The principle thus officially avowed by the society Judge Jay declared had not the remotest connection with the true objects for which the society was formed, nor was it sanctioned by the constitution. "However grievous some women may find the yoke imposed upon them by the opinions usually entertained on the subject," he continued, "that is not the yoke which abolitionists associated to break." The claims now set up by the society in regard to "the rights of women" appeared to him necessarily to involve their participation in the sacred ministry, their exercise of the elective franchise, and their entire independence in the conjugal relation. Irrespective of the soundness of these claims, it did not appear by what right the society called upon its members to support them. Judge Jay contended that "any association for the professed purpose of abolishing negro slavery may with as much propriety prescribe the form of baptism and the Lord's Supper as it may insist that women are authorized to administer these ordinances." Fully convinced that the society as thus managed was exerting an influence not only very injurious to the antislavery cause, but contrary to domestic order and happiness and inconsistent with the precepts of the Gospel, Judge Jay deemed it his duty to sever his connection with it.

In our time, when the admission of women to participation in nearly every form of activity is universally accepted, it may seem extraordinary that the American Antislavery Society should have divided upon such an issue. But what is now a familiar custom was then a strange doctrine, the consequences of which were unknown and were dreaded by conservative people. The abolitionists whose votes admitted women to equal rights with men contended that women were among the most useful and influential workers for the cause and that they should have a corresponding position in the councils of the party. It was denied that active participation in the meetings of the societies was inappropriate to their sex. On the other hand, it was believed by many persons earnestly and usefully engaged in the cause of emancipation that the antislavery society should pursue its end unimpeded and undisturbed by outside issues. The emancipation of woman might be a highly desirable reform, but it should be sought separately from the emancipation of the negro. An individual should be allowed to labour for the slave without being forced to support untried theories regarding woman's rights and the sinfulness of human government.

At this period Judge Jay was especially active with his pen. In 1839 was published his "View of the Action of the Federal Government in Behalf of Slavery." This work was the first effective exposure of the manner in which the United States Government had been used for many years by pro-slavery statesmen to carry out their own ends. Judge Jay showed the shameful position in which the National Government had been placed before the nations of the world when the President and his diplomatic representatives were forced by the Slave Power to demand the return of fugitive slaves and compensation for their loss when shipwreck had allowed them to attain liberty on a foreign shore; when the armies of the United States were sent to Florida at enormous expense to capture alleged runaway private property; when the power of the Government was strained to prevent abolition in Cuba and to introduce slavery into Texas. The efforts to suppress the right of petition and freedom of debate in Congress were thoroughly described. An account, humiliating to every American, was given of the condition of the national capital itself, converted by the fostering protection of the United States Government into the chief slave-market of the Union.

Judge Jay's next publication was entitled, "On the Condition of Free People of Colour in the United States." He showed that they were denied the right to the franchise, to liberty of locomotion, to the lowest employment in the public service; that their education was impeded almost to prohibition and that even their industry was hampered by cruel restrictions. Worst of all, they might at any time be seized and sold into slavery without recourse to law. In 1840 appeared his pamphlet on "The Violation by the House of Representatives of the Right of Petition." These writings had a wide circulation among persons not reached by the ordinary antislavery literature, and their influence was highly beneficial.

Although the woman question was the ostensible

cause of the schism of 1840, there were several other differences which tended quite as much to divide the abolition camp. While the Garrison party continued to depend solely upon moral agitation and opposed all political effort, a numerous and powerful body in the antislavery ranks began to look to the ballot-box as the instrument of reform. In 1840, under the leadership of Gerrit Smith, Alvan Stewart, Myron Holley, Elizur Wright, Joshua Leavitt, and William Goodell, a convention at Albany organized the Liberty party by the nomination of James G. Birney, of Kentucky, for President, and of Thomas Earle, of Pennsylvania, for Vice-President. Out of a total of about two and a half million votes cast at this election, the candidates of the Liberty party received a little over seven thousand. W. H. Harrison, the whig candidate, defeated his democratic opponent, Martin Van Buren. Although the abolition vote was not large, it gave the party great encouragement, and an address was issued congratulating the friends of the slave that a new power to overthrow slavery had been found in "the terse literature of the ballot-box."

Judge Jay's attitude towards the formation of the Liberty party appears in a correspondence which took place between him and Gerrit Smith in July, 1840. "I suppose you have come, as well as myself," wrote Smith, "to the conclusion that whilst American slavery exists our national political parties will be essentially and irrevocably pro-slavery parties, and that abolitionists cannot, therefore, vote consistently for the candidates of such parties. If you have come to this conclusion, you of course admit that we are under the necessity of designating our own candidates for law-makers and that the object of the Freeman's State Convention to be held in Syracuse the first Wednesday in August is proper. Now, when we come together in that convention there is one thing which, next to the blessing of Heaven, we shall need far more than any other. I mean your consent that we shall put you in nomination for governor. Will you enable me to insure the convention of that consent? If you will, you will in so doing render a very great service to our holy cause—a service which I see not how we can well dispense with. If there be anything selfish in your heart, we have, of course, nothing to address to it. We do not expect to elect you, and we are well aware that your nomination would expose you to pro-slavery ridicule and hatred. If you give your consent to the nomination, we know that such consent must proceed from your disinterested and self-sacrificing love for the antislavery cause. Do, my dear sir, give us your name; we can rally about it those who will be dead to the power of any other name."

To this strong appeal Jay gave the following reply:

"I was last evening favoured with your letter of the 20th inst. asking me to consent to be the abolition candidate for governor at the ensuing election. The request implies a confidence in the strength and sincerity of my attachment for the abolition cause that demands my acknowledgments. I cannot now embrace the opportunity afforded by your letter of entering at large into the question of a distinct abolition party; but justice to myself and respect for you induce me to mention some general principles which I think applicable to the present case.

"An abolition political party supposes a union for the election of rulers without regard to the sentiments of the associates or their candidates on any other subject than that of slavery. Of course the party and the rulers elected by them may have the most opposite and irreconcilable opinions on every topic but one of local and national interest; yet it is supposed such discordant materials will form one homogeneous mass. Abolitionists give but little promise of such wonderful unity in the future. I doubt the practicability of forming such a party; and I moreover question whether such a party would be consistent with our obligations as citizens. It is evident that this party could effect its professed object, the abolition of slavery, only in a course of years, and in the meantime it is *to neglect and disregard every other interest.* The party as such can have no opinion and exert no influence either in elections or elsewhere in relation to the trade, the finances, internal improvements, foreign affairs, or the military power of the nation, and no inquiry is to be allowed into the opinions of candidates on these most important topics.

"I fear the very attempt to form such a party will prove injurious to the antislavery cause. It excites dissensions among ourselves. On this point I will not enlarge. It will present in its results a false and disheartening estimate of the number of abolitionists; because as many antislavery men will refuse to support the abolition candidates, the canvass will represent us as far less numerous than we really are.

Moreover, the abolitionists who are thus called out of the political parties can of course exercise no more influence in them. We are depriving the parties of the little salt that keeps them from utter putrefaction. Had the whig abolitionists in the last Legislature been nominated by an abolitionist party they would not have been elected and we should not now have the glorious and blessed jury law.

"I have never approved under present circumstances of any further organized interference by abolitionists with elections than the official questioning of candidates. Under that system every abolitionist might exert a powerful influence merely by withholding his vote, without giving his suffrage for one to whom he was politically opposed. The experiment failed, but by whose fault? Seward and Bradish, Marcy and Tracy, dealt frankly with us. Yet abolitionists made but little difference between the friends and foes. Had Bradish had 20,000 votes more than Seward the conversion of our politicians to abolition would have been general and instantaneous, and slavery would have received an irremediable wound. And can we believe that if abolitionists would not then refrain from voting for the party, they will now consent to vote against it?

"I am very far from thinking that it can never be right and proper to set up abolition candidates without regard to party preferences. Had the question of emancipation been almost equally poised in the British Parliament it would have been patriotic to turn the scale by a temporary abandonment of the contested objects and the election of antislavery members. And so also I can readily conceive of circumstances in which it may be the duty of the abolitionists of a particular State or district to suspend for a time their labours for the slave in order to unite with the friends of temperance to carry some great point. But taking into consideration the existing circumstances of the antislavery cause, I am not clear that the formation of an abolition political party, disregarding all the other interests of the country, is consistent with either duty or policy, and of course it becomes me to decline the request with which you have honoured me. May God enlighten and direct us, and when we cannot think alike may He give us the graces of meekness and charity."

CHAPTER VI.

JUDGE JAY CONTINUES TO SUPPORT THE ANTISLAVERY CAUSE BY HIS ADVICE AND WRITINGS.—IN CONSEQUENCE OF HIS OPINIONS HE IS DEPRIVED OF HIS SEAT ON THE BENCH.—HIS VISIT TO EUROPE.—HIS VIEWS ON THE LIBERTY PARTY.—ON THE ANNEXATION OF TEXAS. —HIS "REVIEW OF THE MEXICAN WAR."—HIS ADVOCACY OF INTERNATIONAL ARBITRATION AS A REMEDY FOR WAR.—HIS WORK IN THE EPISCOPAL CHURCH.

AFTER the division in the ranks of the antislavery societies in 1840, Judge Jay ceased to take an active part in their proceedings, preferring to support the cause independently by his writings. But he was continually applied to by the societies to assist them by his advice, to give legal opinions on the positions which they wished to take, and to prepare documents which required special judgment and ability.

In April, 1842, Jay prepared an address to the British Antislavery Society, at the request of Mrs. Lydia Maria Child, who wrote on behalf of the American Antislavery Society. A little later, again by request of Mrs. Child, he gave a legal opinion on the advisability of carrying to the Supreme Court the cases of three men who had been condemned in

Missouri to twelve years' imprisonment for aiding slaves to escape.

He continued his membership in the American and Foreign Antislavery Society in New York. Here he laboured unceasingly to keep the society fast to its declared purpose, and to prevent it from adding new doctrines and objects which he believed must result in further divisions injurious to the cause.

In April, 1841, he wrote on this subject to Lewis Tappan:

"I am glad the society will not be concerned in establishing a missionary station in Africa. The great vice of our antislavery societies has been, and is, meddling with things they have no right to meddle with, and this they have done on a most vicious principle, that the end sanctifies the means. In general, abolitionists mean well; but they grievously mistake when they think themselves authorized to pursue, in their associated capacity, whatever benevolent or religious plan they individually approve. They unite for certain specified purposes, and receive money expressly to forward those purposes; and to employ their associated influence or their common funds for other distinct purposes is not, in my opinion, consistent with strict morality."

In August, 1841, Judge Jay was requested by the Executive Committee of the American and Foreign Antislavery Society to allow his name to be announced as a regular contributor to the society's organ, the *Reporter*. He took this opportunity to repeat his warnings against the departure of the abolitionists from the line of action which they had marked out for themselves in the early days of the agitation.

"As an abolitionist I have deeply deplored the dissensions which have marred our harmony and almost annihilated our moral influence; and I have constantly and resolutely abstained, as far as my sense of duty would permit me, from aggravating those dissensions by partaking in them. The obvious tendency of the *announcement* contemplated by your resolution is to impress the public with the belief that the gentlemen who are held forth as the future contributors to the *Reporter* maintain the principles and approve the course of that paper. Such an impression, so far as regards myself, would be most strictly accurate were the principles and course of the paper to continue such as they have hitherto been. To the American and Foreign Antislavery Society I did fondly look as a refuge for such abolitionists as had been expelled from the old society by the faithlessness of those who converted it into an instrument for spreading other than antislavery doctrines. I did, notwithstanding past experience, regard the constitution of the new society as affording a guarantee that its members would not be required to support any other principles and measures than such as were indicated in that instrument. In consequence of this belief I did not decline office in the society, and I aided in defraying the expenses and in filling the columns of the *Reporter*. The paper was conducted with ability and honesty, promised to exert a happy influence in restoring peace and harmony to our ranks. The society was pledged by its constitution 'carefully to abstain from all the machinery of party political arrangements in effecting the objects,' and the *Reporter* faithfully conformed itself to this pledge. But in the very last number we are informed that at the last meeting a vote of the society, '*nearly unanimous,*' was taken in favour of striking this pledge from the constitution, but that inasmuch as the notice required by Article X. had not been given, the amendment was not *constitutionally* adopted. The pledge is therefore virtually, although not formally, withdrawn; and we have every reason to believe that at the next meeting it will be expunged from the constitution. It is therefore obvious that the society, instead of being a rallying point for abolitionists, is henceforth to be a mere partisan organization, excluding from its fellowship multitudes of honest, zealous, and consistent abolitionists because they cannot adopt the maxim now promulgated in certain quarters, that the friends of immediate emancipation should labour to secure for themselves all the loaves and fishes in the gift of the republic—the power and emoluments of *every office*, from that of President of the United States to that of Path Master of a ward district. The vote of the society just mentioned is tantamount to a declaration that it will as soon as possible employ all the machinery of party political arrangement for the exclusive elevation of abolitionists to political power. This is not an object for which I have associated with abolitionists, nor is it one in which I intend to co-operate with them. But the *Reporter*, I am bound to believe, will be used as an instrument to effect this object, because I am bound to believe that the official organ of the society will not fail to advocate and pursue its avowed policy. Hence I cannot and ought not to give it in advance my confidence and countenance by complying with the request with which you have honoured me.

"I have thus frankly stated my sentiments without intending to impeach the motives of others, and without meaning to assume a hostile attitude towards the friends and supporters of what is denominated the Third party. With that party I cannot conscientiously and consistently unite, but I have purposely abstained from publicly mingling in the controversies to which it has given rise, and I have now expressed my dissent from it only because I could not otherwise explain my refusal of your polite invitation.

"In justice to myself, permit me to remark that my opinions on slavery and abolition have undergone no change, and that every principle I have ever avowed as an abolitionist is still cherished by me with no other difference than possibly a stronger conviction than formerly of its truth and importance.

"That we may all be guided by wisdom from above and be enabled not merely to break the bonds of the slaves, but in our conduct to adorn our Christian profession, is my fervent wish."

The antislavery societies, by the admission into their proceedings of projected reforms having no connection with their ostensible object, had gradually become divided and weakened. Jay had protested unceasingly against this course, but the tendency had been irresistible. "Our antislavery societies," he wrote in 1846, "are, for the most part, virtually defunct. Antislavery conventions are whatever the leaders present happen to be; sometimes disgustingly irreligious, and very often Jacobinical and disorganizing; and frequently proscriptive of such of their brethren who will not consent to render abolition a mere instrument for effecting certain political changes having no relation whatever to slavery."

The antislavery societies had accomplished the noble and seemingly hopeless task of arousing the national conscience from its lethargy. Their labours had started and given irresistible impulse to a movement on behalf of the slave which was not to rest until emancipation was attained. But the active conduct of this movement was now passing from their hands into the domain of politics. The contest had become a national issue, to be fought out in legislative halls and to be determined at the polls.

In August, 1843, the national convention of the Liberty party was held at Buffalo. This convention was more largely attended than the first, every free State excepting New Hampshire having sent delegates. James G. Birney was again nominated for President, and Thomas Morris, of Ohio, for Vice-President. The canvass was carried on with great vigour and spirit. The Birney vote in 1843 showed a large increase, amounting to 60,000. It caused the election of Polk and gave to the abolitionists the balance of power in New York and Michigan.

Judge Jay had never considered himself as belonging to either the Whig or the Democratic party. He believed that his judicial position should debar him from active partisanship. Above all, his disapproval of the policy adopted by both political parties towards the slavery question disinclined him to be a member of either. His attitude towards the Liberty party, on its formation in 1840, was set forth in the letter written to Gerrit Smith declining the nomination for governor, which was quoted at length in the last chapter. Judge Jay then doubted the expediency of a separate political party making abolition its article of faith and test of membership. But as events proceeded, as both the great parties seemed irrevocably pledged to the support of slavery, above all, as both favoured the annexation of Texas, Jay became a pronounced and active member of the Liberty party.

He viewed the annexation proceedings with horror, as the death-knell of emancipation and as a scheme of wicked injustice which must react injuriously upon the whole nation. In March, 1843, he wrote to Dr. H. J. Bowditch, of Boston : " The full and entire triumph of the antislavery cause is near and certain, provided that Texas is kept out of the Union. On this point are centred all my fears. I am not disheartened by the corruption of politicians, nor the deathlike apathy of the community, so long as we remain independent of the renegade republic. Give us time and we can arouse the community from its stupor, we can change public opinion, and politicians will bellow aloud for abolition the moment they find it popular. The danger is that before this change is effected the slaveholders will demand the annexation of Texas as the price of the presidency and that one or more of the candidates will consent to pay it."

When Birney was nominated in 1843, Jay wrote to Gerrit Smith: "I congratulate you upon this result. Birney is a man for whom Christians and patriots can consistently vote. He shall have my cordial support. In my opinion, the selection is creditable to the Liberty party, and if it continues to give us candidates of this character, it will be a blessing to our country . . . To that party I shall be true so far, and so far only, as it shall be true to itself. May God direct its measures for the protection of our own rights and for the ultimate liberation of the slave."

Judge Jay was as anxious that the Liberty party should keep faithfully to its antislavery purpose as he had been in the case of the antislavery societies. He believed that the party must end in failure if it allowed extraneous and dividing policies to be admitted to its platform. On this subject he wrote in September, 1845, to Henry B. Stanton, who had invited him to a convention in Boston:

"Notwithstanding the annexation of Texas, great good may result from the Liberty party, provided it be faithful to itself, and be wisely conducted. Hence I am distressed by whatever threatens to impair its integrity and usefulness. You are not ignorant, I presume, of the strenuous efforts now making to change its character and to convert it from an antislavery party into one for matters and things in general.

"It is proposed by men of talents, energy, and influence that the party shall in future maintain:

"That the Federal Government has the Constitutional power to abolish slavery in the *States*.

"That the clergy shall be subject to all the burdens and enjoy all the privileges of other citizens. This is aimed at the clergy of New York who are not eligible to office, but exempted, to a great extent, from taxation. No man is hereafter to be acknowledged to belong to the Liberty party unless he objects to the State showing any indulgence to the ministers of religion. They must be enrolled in the militia, and, like others, called out to work on the highway.

"That custom-houses be abolished, and with them all protective duties.

"That the salaries of the President and Congressmen be reduced.

"That the legal profession is a privileged caste and should be abolished.

"That the public lands be given away.

"That all monopolies, by which I understand incorporated companies, banks, railroads, etc., be abolished.

"That women should exercise the right of suffrage and be eligible to office, etc., etc., etc.

"It is needless to say that if these tests of membership of the Liberty party be adopted, we shall drive from us all whose judgment or whose consciences revolt at them, while those who remain in the party will regard the removal of slavery as a very subordinate object of their labours. My purpose of troubling you with this letter is to suggest to you the expediency of the convention adopting a resolution in which, without alluding to the efforts making to change the character of the party, it shall declare that the sole objects of the party are the abolition of slavery, the deliverance of the Federal Government from its influence, and the elevation of the coloured race to equal rights with the whites; and inviting all who approve of those objects to co-operate with us, whatever may be their opinion on questions of State or national policy."

At the Liberty party convention held at Newburg in October, 1845, Judge Jay was unanimously nominated as a candidate for Senator. In his letter accepting the nomination, he took occasion again to urge the exclusion of irrelevant subjects from the platform of the party.

"Recent circumstances induce me to accompany my acceptance of this nomination with some remarks. Attempts are making to render the Liberty party subservient to other objects than the overthrow of slavery and the elevation of the coloured people. To these attempts I can lend no aid. While I most explicitly accord to every abolitionist the right of expressing his own opinions on every political and religious subject, I as explicitly deny the right, and shall strenuously resist the attempt, to make me and other members responsible for opinions not necessarily involved in the great objects for the attainment of which the party was formed. In the pursuit of those objects I will cordially and honestly co-operate with others from whose sentiments I dissent; but I cannot co-operate with them in promoting religious and political changes which I believe to be wrong, in order to increase the influence and hasten the triumph of the Liberty party. To do so would be to act upon the principle, as wicked and detestable as slavery itself, that the end justifies the means. The fact that many good men who unite in abhorrence of slavery entertain conflicting views of the expediency and morality of various proposed reforms seems to me a sufficient reason why the Liberty party should not permit itself to be distracted by the other questions which agitate the community, and which in truth are of but little moment compared with the great evil with which we are struggling."

In 1846 Jay wrote again on this subject : "I shall leave the Liberty party whenever it makes abolition a pack-horse to carry favourite measures unconnected with slavery, whether those measures are of whig or democratic origin."

Early in the year 1843 the antislavery opinions and labours of Judge Jay caused the loss of his seat on the bench of Westchester County, which he had occupied for more than twenty-five years with such general approval as to cause his steady reappointment term after term by governors of the State who were his political opponents. The circumstances of his removal are described in a letter which he wrote to Mr. Minot Mitchell, in May, 1843:

"I thank you for your friendly letter in relation to my removal from the bench. The loss of an office which I had held for about a quarter of a century (and which I had contemplated resigning in the course of the present year) is not a matter of personal regret. My motive in holding for so long a time a situation which subjected me to no little inconvenience and yielded no emolument was a desire to be useful, and a belief that I could exert on the bench a wholesome moral influence. How far that belief was well founded is for others to decide. To myself, it is grateful to know that my official conduct, whatever mistakes I may have made, has been pure, unbiased by personal partialities, and uninfluenced by any fear except that of my Maker.

"To the gentlemen of the Westchester bar generally, as well as to yourself in particular, I am deeply indebted for the uniform kindness and courtesy with which I have been treated; and had I known at the December term that we were not to meet again, I would have embraced the opportunity of publicly acknowledging my obligations to them, and of bidding them an affectionate farewell.

"Under the circumstances of the case, it would be an affectation of humility to ascribe my loss of office to any dissatisfaction with my official conduct on the part of the bar or the public. The *New York Plebeian*, amid all its vituperative clamour for my dismissal, does not even hint a charge against me as a judge, and the editor of the *Westchester Herald*, notwithstanding his blind devotion to his party, bears a flattering testimony to my ability as a 'jurist,' and admits that my 'moral worth' is not questioned, as he believes, 'by any man in the country.'

"Nor have I been proscribed on account of my political opinions. Those opinions belong to the old Washington school—I have never concealed them; and they are the same now as they were when I received office from Governors Tompkins, Clinton, Throop, and Marcy, and when President Jackson tendered to me an important and lucrative appointment.

"For twenty years or more I have had no connection with party politics, and have attended no party meeting. It appeared to me unbecoming a judge to be a political partisan; and I, moreover, observed so much profligacy, venality, and hypocritical profession in both parties, that I could not conscientiously identify myself with either. I have for years voted for those I believed to be the most honest of the candidates offered for my suffrage, without regard to the party dogmas they professed.

"That the people of Westchester had lost their confidence in me and wished me to descend from the bench is not pretended. On the contrary, I have the most abundant and gratifying proofs of the correctness of your remark, that my removal has occasioned in the county, with all political parties, unusual dissatisfaction and complaint.

"If, then, my removal has been effected contrary to the wishes of the county, and not because I lacked in ability or integrity, nor even on account of my politics, it becomes a matter of public interest to inquire with what motives and with what views the chief magistrate of New York dispenses the patronage intrusted to him by the constitution for the good of the State.

"Governor Bouck has, in this instance, as in another far more important, only acted as the instrument of a faction which, while prating about *equal rights*, is ever ready and eager to barter the welfare, honour, and freedom of the North for Southern votes.

"You may recollect that previous to my last appointment I was permitted to hold over for a year after my term of office had expired. This extraordinary delay in filling a vacancy on the bench was not the result of accident or inadvertency. It arose from doubts entertained by the leaders at Albany whether the party would gain more at the South than it would lose in Westchester by my removal. Mr. Van Buren was then a candidate for the presidency, and I was shown a confidential letter from one of his particular friends at Albany to an influential democrat of this county, discussing the expediency of my removal. The letter was put into my hands by the gentleman to whom it was addressed. It was admitted by the writer that my conduct as a judge was irreproachable, and that there were no other objections to my reappointment than my antislavery sentiments. My only fault in the eyes of this champion of equal rights was that I was opposed to converting men and women into beasts of burden. Still, he was apprehensive that my removal for *such* a cause might savour of persecution for *abstract opinions;* in other words, might be unpopular ; and he wished to know what the party in Westchester deemed most expedient. After a year's deliberation and hesitation, I was reappointed. Mr. Van Buren is again a candidate, but *now* he has a Southern democrat for a competitor ; and his party in the State being so strong that he can well afford to risk a little dissatisfaction in Westchester, it is deemed prudent to propitiate the demon of slavery by offering a victim, however humble, on his altar. The *Plebeian*, devoted to Mr. Van Buren's election, avowed with unblushing frankness that my reappointment would be calculated to prejudice the Democratic party 'in the eyes of our Southern brethren.'

"Thus, it seems that in order to elevate Mr. Van Buren to the presidency the magistrates of the free, sovereign, and independent State of New York are to be selected with reference to the good pleasure of Southern slaveholders.

"Pardon, my dear sir, the egotism of this letter. I have been compelled to speak of myself in order to expose the canting profligacy of our demagogues, and to illustrate one of the numberless accursed influences of slavery. This abhorred system, which in the South makes merchandise of the souls and bodies of men, is at the same time trafficking in the politics, the religion, and the liberties of the North, and putrefying whatever it touches. Against this system I have contended, as did my father before me, and the leisure Governor Bouck has given me shall be faithfully devoted to a continuance of the warfare."

The " leisure " given to him by Governor Bouck had first to be used by Jay in an attempt to restore his health, which for several years had been failing. In the autumn of 1843 he determined upon a visit to Egypt, and on the 1st of November he sailed from New York in the " Victoria," of 1100 tons, accompanied by his wife and his daughters Maria and Augusta. After a short visit to London, the party sailed from

Southampton for Malta in the "Great Liverpool" of the Oriental Line, with passengers and mail bound to India. At Malta Jay was interested in meeting the famous wit, scholar, and diplomatist, John Hookham Frere, who entertained him at his house outside the walls of the city.

While in England, Jay had been requested by John Beaumont, on behalf of the British and Foreign Anti-slavery Society, to take charge of a quantity of anti-slavery tracts printed in the Arabic language, and to insure their distribution. After his arrival in Cairo, Jay gave packages of the tracts to several persons whose facilities for distributing them in Egypt were greater than his own. Others he disposed of himself. "During the short time I was in Egypt," he said in a letter, "I distributed tracts in the slave market, in the bazaars, in a public coffee-house, in the hotels, and to persons in the streets." And he was much struck with the fact that what he could do peacefully in Egypt, in a portion of his own country would have endangered his life.

On his return home, Jay visited Paris, and while there communicated to the Duc de Broglie the motives of the Southern statesmen in seeking the annexation of Texas, and made no secret of his hope that France would oppose the proceedings.*

---

* During Judge Jay's absence in Europe a striking anti-annexation Texas meeting was held at the Tabernacle in New York, on the 24th of April, 1844. It had been called by members of the King, Duer, Townsend, Goodhue, Sedgwick, Field, Griswold, and Hyslop families and many leading merchants of New York. The call was subsequently pre-

The events leading up to the annexation of Texas and the Mexican War were followed by Jay with the closest attention. The injustice and cruelty with which Mexico was treated throughout these proceedings by the United States Government excited his warmest indignation. He was deeply grieved at events which seemed to postpone indefinitely the emancipation of the slaves; his fears were aroused for the security of free institutions in the North by the great impetus given to the Southern spirit of domination. But above all he felt the disgrace incurred by his own country in forcing upon a weak and friendly power a desolating war for the sole object of wresting from it a territory to be peopled by slaves. The result of Jay's minute knowledge of this dark page in American history was embodied in a volume entitled "A Review of the Causes and Consequences of the Mexican War," which was published

sented by John Jay to the New York Historical Society, for preservation in its records. A letter was read from Chancellor Kent denouncing the annexation of Texas without the consent of Mexico as a breach of national faith which would be universally condemned. Speeches were made by Theodore Sedgwick and D. D. Field. But the most imposing feature of the manifestation was the presence in the chair of Albert Gallatin, the last survivor of Jefferson's cabinet, who, despite his age and infirmities, had been carried to the meeting to protest in his own name and in that of his historic chief against so flagrant a violation of national honour and public faith. The appeal of Gallatin for a time promised to be successful. Van Buren, whose views had been doubtful, wrote, under its influence, his letter to Hammett objecting to annexation. But an annexation meeting was held in Richmond to counteract that at New York, and when the Democratic Convention met at Baltimore an adroit change of policy in regard to nominations displaced Van Buren and nominated Polk.

in 1849. In this searching "Review" Jay exposed the parentage of the movement for the acquisition of Texas in the desire of the South to extend the territory devoted to slavery, with the twofold object of creating a new market for slave-breeders and of giving to the slave States an overwhelming control of Congress. He traced the devious paths of intrigue by which a rebellion was fomented in Texas by Americans settled there for that express purpose; the encouragement and aid given secretly to the rebels by the United States; the recognition of their independence; and finally the subterfuges adopted to achieve the annexation in violation of international rights and the Constitution itself. Jay set forth plainly the fact that hostilities were begun by the United States troops; he described the military operations by which a weak and defenceless people were reduced to consent to a dismemberment of their country; he showed the enormous cost in life and money involved in this war undertaken to furnish a new market for slaves and new power to slaveholders. Jay's "Review of the Mexican War" is a contribution to the history of the country which students cannot afford to pass unread. The views expressed in it are painful to patriotism for the reason that they are dictated by the pure patriotism which would make known the whole truth as a warning to posterity.

The book on the Mexican War was written originally for the American Peace Society, which had offered a prize for the best work on the subject. The committee appointed to pass judgment on the dissertations presented in competition awarded the prize to Jay's book on condition that he should expunge from it all "general censures on the Whig party." Jay refused to comply with this condition and the prize went to another. But the Peace Society recognized that the value of Jay's book lay in its impartial character and caused it to be published as the exposition of the society's views.

As nearly all the newspapers of both parties had supported the war, they were loth to notice a book which placed the object of their encomiums in so unpleasant a light. But many private letters were received by Jay which showed him that he had the approval of the best minds. Joshua R. Giddings wrote: "Thanks be to Him who rules the destiny of nations that we have among us competent and faithful men who possess the moral courage to stand forth and chronicle, in the language of truth, the barbarities of which the nation is guilty. The history of this age will speak to those who come after facts which will cause our descendants to blush. Your 'Review of the Mexican War' is faithful and just. . . . In writing it you have performed a service to your country and to mankind infinitely greater than was ever performed by any military officer."

"Every portion of it," wrote Charles Francis Adams, "commands my unqualified assent. That in the course of God's providence good may be ultimately educed out of evil is the only compensating reflection which we can draw from the observation of so much wrong. It may be that out of the very measures so wickedly devised to sustain a system of crime may come the means by which it will be overthrown. That your book will do great service in combining and perpetuating the evidence bearing upon this portion of American history, I do not for a moment doubt. It is my profound conviction that there never was a more wicked and unjustifiable war, promoted by one party and connived at by the other, than the late war with Mexico."

The prevention of war was a subject which had occupied the mind of Judge Jay for a number of years. The result of his reflections was that system of international arbitration which has become since his death so efficacious a method of settling international disputes. A pamphlet entitled "War and Peace: the Evils of the First and a Plan for Preserving the Last" was still in manuscript in his desk when, in 1841, Joseph Sturge, the celebrated English philanthropist, visited Bedford. Jay read the pamphlet to Sturge, who was so much struck by the work that he embodied a portion of it in a book which he published on his return to England. The views of Jay attracted the attention of the English Peace Society, who published the whole pamphlet in London in 1842. Jay's plan for the prevention of war was exceedingly simple. It provided that a stipulation should be made in every treaty that future international differences should be referred first to arbitration, to attempt a peaceful settlement. The idea was heartily approved by Cobden, who wrote to Judge Jay: "If your government is prepared to insert an arbitration clause in the pending treaties I am persuaded that it will be accepted by our government." The scheme of arbitration thus proposed by Jay, and supported by Joseph Sturge and his friends of the English Peace Society, was approved by peace congresses held in Brussels in 1848, in Paris in 1849, and in London in 1851. Having thus attracted general attention, it was recommended by protocol No. 23 of the Congress of Paris held in 1856 after the Crimean War, which protocol was unanimously adopted by the plenipotentiaries of France, Austria, Great Britain, Prussia, Russia, Sardinia, and Turkey. These governments declared their wish that the States between which any serious misunderstanding might arise should, before appealing to arms, have recourse, as far as circumstances might allow, to the good offices of a friendly power. The honour of the introduction of this measure in the first Congress belongs to Lord Clarendon, whose services had been solicited by Joseph Sturge and Henry Richard. It was subsequently referred to by Lord Derby as worthy of immortal honour. Lord Malmsbury pronounced it an act "important to civilization and to the security of the peace of Europe." The protocol was afterwards approved by all the other powers to which it was referred, more than forty in number. The plan thus suggested by Judge Jay for the prevention of war bore fruit during his life, and was destined in after-years to become established in the mind of the civilized world as the true remedy for the greatest scourge of nations.*

Judge Jay was an earnest and active member of the Episcopal Church, but he was never blind to its imperfections. He deplored as much as any man the countenance given by the church to slavery, but he believed that reformation must and would come from within. He had no sympathy with the "come-outers." Concerning them he wrote in 1846 : "Infidelity is now vigorously availing itself of the conduct of the clergy in relation to this subject to assail the blessed religion of which they are the ministers. A sect is forming who profess to believe that the church is so corrupted by slavery that good men are required to separate from her. These people call themselves 'come-outers.' Lecturers are enlisted in their service, and the clergy, as identified with the cause of human bondage, are daily held up to public detestation as heartless hypocrites." Jay would not deny the justice with which the attacks on the clergy were made, and he laboured to place the church where it belonged, in the front rank of the great humanitarian movement. To his efforts were largely due the admission of coloured clergy to the conventions of the church, and the gradual abolition of that spirit of caste which prevented a white clergyman from recognizing a black one as fit to deliberate with him on

* The later history of international arbitration is set forth by Sir Lyon Playfair in the *North American Review* for December, 1890.

matters relating to their common religion. To destroy this race hatred, so contrary to the spirit of Christianity, and to arouse the church to its duty of active opposition to slavery, were Jay's constant endeavours in the conventions of the church. His pen also was frequently occupied with the same subject. His "Letter to Bishop Ives" of North Carolina was a severe yet just arraignment of clergymen who justified slavery from the Scriptures, and it exposed the wickedness of their course in language and with arguments to which they and their sympathizers were unable to reply.

When a "History of the American Church," by Samuel Wilberforce, was published in England, there was naturally in America much curiosity to see the work. Two American publishers announced their intention of reprinting it. But time passed and no reprint appeared. The explanation is given in the words of Jay : "The author of the 'History' in the course of his work advances certain doctrines on the subject of 'slavery' and of 'caste in the church' which it is thought inconvenient to discuss, and which cannot be admitted in this republic without sealing the condemnation·of almost every Christian sect among us and overwhelming our own church with shame and confusion. There are, it is to be feared, but few among our twelve hundred clergymen who, on reading the 'History,' would not find their consciences whispering, 'Thou art the man,' and who would not be anxious to conceal the volume from their parishioners. Hence its suppression." Jay was determined that the truths regarding the Episcopal Church in America set forth by the celebrated Dr. Wilberforce should not be quite unattainable by the clergy and laity especially concerned. In 1846 he caused those passages of the "History" relating to slavery to be printed, and introduced them with forcible remarks of his own in the pamphlet entitled "A Reproof of the American Church by the Bishop of Oxford."

CHAPTER VII.

UNPOPULARITY OF THE ABOLITIONISTS.—THE COMPROMISES OF 1850 AND THE FUGITIVE-SLAVE LAW.—JAY'S REPLY TO WEBSTER'S 7th OF MARCH SPEECH.—THE ATTITUDE OF THE EPISCOPAL CHURCH.—THE ABROGATION OF THE MISSOURI COMPROMISE.—DISUNION.

THE prospect was dark for the antislavery cause in 1850. Its friends had increased steadily in numbers and in earnestness. But the Slave Power had mustered all its forces in an aggressive campaign which aimed to make slavery a national instead of a local institution, to introduce it into territory hitherto free, and to browbeat the North into submission to every demand of the slaveholder. The compromise measures adopted this year in Congress—above all, the Fugitive-Slave Law—marked the successful advance of arrogant Southern dictation. In the North, the dislike of antislavery men and the willingness to satisfy the South at the expense of conscience was expressed in such scenes as the attack of the Rynders mob on the meeting of the American Antislavery Society in New York and the passive attitude towards it adopted by the authorities. Although the plan of putting down the abolitionists by force had proved impracticable, no efforts were spared to make their lives uncomfortable by the attacks of the press and by the pressure of social disapproval. " Our politicians," wrote Jay to Charles Sumner, " may pride themselves on their adroitness in pandering to popular prejudices, and in acquiring power and influence by seasonable changes of opinion and conduct. But a day is coming when their motives and actions will be judged by a very different tribunal than public opinion, and when a single act of benevolence, a single sacrifice of personal consideration to the cause of truth, will outweigh a whole life of obsequiousness and political trickery.

"The truths we advocate are unpalatable to the two extremes of society. We shock the coarse, vulgar prejudices of the rabble, while the disinterested benevolence we profess is to them an enigma to be solved only by the imputation of fanaticism. At the same time we disturb the tranquil consciences of the rich, thwart the calculations of politicans, and interrupt the harmony subsisting between our merchants and their Southern customers. Hence the upper classes look upon us as impertinent and exceedingly ungenteel, and unfit to move in the higher circles. I cannot tell how far your personal experience coincides with mine, but *I* know whereof I affirm. I have advanced no ultra-fanatical doctrines in politics or religion. On the subject of slavery I have but reiterated the opinions of many of the best and greatest men in England and in our own country. I have advocated no congressional action except such as Mr. Webster, in his better days, pronounced constitutional, and I have condemned all forcible resistance to the Fugitive-Slave Law. Yet solely on account of my antislavery efforts, I find myself nearly insulated in society."

The Compromise measures of 1850 were repulsive and disheartening to the antislavery men in the North. And no circumstance connected with them was more discouraging than the change of front made by Daniel Webster—his abandonment of the Wilmot Proviso and his concession to the Southern demand for the extension of slavery into the new territory acquired by the Mexican War. Webster's speech of the 7th of March was answered by Judge Jay in a letter to the *Evening Post* of March 20th, and was afterwards published as a pamphlet and widely circulated. In this letter Jay recalled the eloquent and positive declaration of Webster made in the Senate on August 10, 1848, after New Mexico and California had been acquired:

"My opposition to the increase of slavery in this country, or to the increase of slave representation, is general and universal. It has no reference to the lines of latitude or points of the compass. I shall oppose all such extension at all times and under all circumstances, even against all inducements, against all supposed limitation of great interests, against all combinations, against all compromises."

These words were contrasted by Jay with Webster's present excuse for abandoning opposition to the extension of slavery on the ground that the laws of "physical geography" made slavery impossible in the new territory and to forbid its existence there was merely "to re-enact the will of God."

"To what," asked Jay, "did this solemn, emphatic, unqualified asservation refer? Did he then know that there was a foot of territory in the United States over which it was morally and physically impossible to extend slavery? Was he promising in these impressive terms to oppose what he was conscious would never be attempted? Did he make this pledge before his country with a mental reservation to unite hereafter with General Cass and the slaveholders in denouncing and scorning the Proviso? Did he mean to deceive his own party? Did he desire to keep up an angry agitation throughout the nation for electioneering purposes, and did he thus intimate his belief in the danger of the extension of slavery and slave representation, when he well knew that the fiat of the Almighty had rendered such extension impossible? Was he then acquainted with the law of physical geography which would render the Proviso 'a re-enactment of the will of God?' And did he purposely conceal the secret of this law in his own breast, when by revealing it he might have stilled the raging billows of popular passion which threatened to ingulf the Union? To suppose all this would be to impute to Mr. Webster a degree of trickery and turpitude rarely paralleled even among politicians. Hence we are bound to assume that the law of nature on which he *now* relies is a recent discovery, subsequent at least to the 10th August, 1848. It is, however, extraordinary that a gentleman of his acquirements did not sooner become acquainted with '*this law of physical geography—the law of the formation of the earth, that settles forever, beyond all terms of human enactment, that slavery cannot exist in California or New Mexico.*' It is to be regretted that Mr. Webster did not condescend to demonstrate the existence of this law and to explain the mode of its operation. He indeed tells us that our new territories are 'Asiatic in their formation and scenery'; but this fact does not prove his law, since slavery has existed for ages amid the scenery of Asia; it exists in the deserts of Africa, has existed in every country of Europe, and now exists in the frozen regions of Russia. This law, moreover, must have been enacted by the Creator since 1824, or its operation must have been suspended in deference to the Spanish government; for under that government negro slavery did exist in California and New Mexico, and it ceased in 1824, not by the 'law of physical geography,' but by a Mexican edict. Thousands of slaves are employed in the mines of Brazil, and Mr. Webster does not explain how his law forbids their employment in the mines of California. . . .

"He pays a sorry compliment to the common sense of the people in offering to them at the eleventh hour a new and unheard-of law of 'physical geography,' together with the 'Asiatic scenery and formation' of the conquered territories, as an *excuse* for violating the faith he had plighted in behalf of the Proviso. He has shocked the moral sense of a large portion of the community by giving in advance his sanction to the Fugitive-Slave Law, which makes the liberty or bondage of a citizen depend on the affidavit of a slaveholder and the judgment of a post-master—a law which converts sympathy for guiltless misery into crime, and threatens to tenant our jails with our most estimable men and women. But Mr. Webster underrates the intelligence and sensibilities of the masses. Relying on the Southern affinities of our commercial cities, on the subserviency of politicians, on the discipline of party, and on his own great influence, Mr. Webster looks *down* upon the people; but the time is probably not far distant when the people will cease to look up to him. Parties will accept of any leaders who can acquire for them the spoils of the day, but in the political history of our country the people have never placed their affections upon any man in whose stability and consistency they did not confide."

To give such assistance as he could to a fugitive slave had always been regarded by Judge Jay as a duty. "The slaveholders," he had written, "with their accustomed impudence and mendacity, apply the term *theft* to the humane and Christian efforts to assist a slave in escaping from his home of bondage. In their sense of the expression, I glory in being a slave-stealer, and I inculcate upon my children the duty, the Christian duty, of this kind of theft." He had sheltered and aided many runaways at his home at Bedford, and his will contained a bequest of a thousand dollars to be used for this purpose. His son John gave his services as a lawyer constantly and successfully to prevent the return of fugitive slaves.

When the Fugitive-Slave Bill became a law Judge Jay was applied to by many individuals, societies, and periodicals to give his views concerning it. "The law," he said in a private letter, "is an outrage upon the Constitution of our country and the precepts of our religion. It is a burlesque on justice and on all the acknowledged rules of evidence in the trial of issues. The demand it makes upon individual citizens to aid in hunting and enslaving their fellow-men is diabolical. I have made up my mind to suffer imprisonment and the spoiling of my goods rather than hazard my soul by rendering any active obedience to this sinful law. It is horrible that so many of our fashionable cotton divines are now preaching up the supremacy of human law and virtually dethroning Him whose ambassadors they profess to be."

"In my opinion, every Northern slave-catcher is a base man, and every lawyer who takes reward against the innocent is a disgrace to a noble profession. I myself shall offer no forcible resistance against the execution of this most wicked law, but I trust that, through the grace of God, I would go to the scaffold sooner than obey it."

Concerning the constitutionality of the law, Judge Jay wrote to Josiah Quincy: "The fugitive-slave clause in the Constitution is of course obligatory, but there is a wide distinction between the fugitive-slave *clause* and the fugitive-slave *law*. The Constitution gives no power to Congress to legislate on the subject, but imposes on the States the obligation of rendition. Chief-Justice Hornblower, of New York, and Chancellor Walworth, of New York, long since pronounced the fugitive law of '93 unconstitutional on this very ground."

The demoralization caused by the execution of the law was described by Jay in a letter to Gerrit Smith: "It is scoundrelizing our people. Cruelty and injustice are cultivated as virtues, Christian love and sympathy with human suffering are treated as prejudices to be conquered, and zeal in hunting slaves is made the test of patriotism and of fitness for office. But the most diabolical effect of the law is the competition it has excited among our politicians to offer the blood of their fellow-citizens in exchange for Southern votes."

To a committee of free coloured men who asked Judge Jay's advice regarding the propriety of arming themselves to prevent being kidnapped under the law, he said: "Most deeply do I sympathize with you in your unhappy state. With your wives and children, you are now placed at the disposal of any villain who is ready to perjure himself for the price you will bring in the human shambles of the South. With less ceremony and trouble than a man can impound his neighbour's ox, you may be metamorphosed from a citizen of the State of New York into a beast of burden on a Southern plantation. On leaving your house in the morning you may be enticed into another, where one of the newly appointed commissioners, after reading one affidavit, made a thousand miles off, and another that you are the person named in the first, or on the bare oath of the kidnapper himself, may inform you, to your amazement and horror, that you are a *slave*. The fetters previously prepared are placed on your limbs, and in a few minutes you are travelling with railroad velocity to a Southern market. Never again will you behold your wife and children, nor will any tidings from them ever reach your ear. The remainder of your life is to be one of toil and stripes. . . . Yet," he continued, "leave, I beseech you, the pistol and the bowie-knife to Southern ruffians and their Northern mercenaries. That this law will lead to bloodshed I take for granted, but let it be the blood of the innocent, not of the guilty. If anything can arouse the torpid conscience of the North, it will be our streets stained with human blood shed by the slave-catchers."

The Fugitive-Slave Law, in Jay's opinion, was the natural sequence to the attempt to put down the antislavery movement by force: "For years, most strenuous efforts, prompted by commercial and political views, were made to deprive the opponents of slavery of their constitutional privileges by lawless violence. The right of petition was suspended, the freedom of debate interrupted, the sanctity of the post-office violated, public meetings dispersed, printing-presses destroyed, furious mobs excited, churches sacked, private houses gutted, and even murder perpetrated. All this violation of rights was regarded with complacency by many who had much at stake, so long as abolitionists alone were the victims. But the spirit of aggression thus raised and fostered is seeking new subjects on which to exercise its power. 'Gentlemen of property and standing' are now beginning to feel alarmed about socialism, anti-rentism, agrarianism, etc. Hence, of late we hear much of the importance of conservatism, as it is called. The political movements of the last few months seem to indicate that our landlords and cotton lords and merchant princes regard an alliance with the aristocracy of the South as at least in some degree a security against the violation of vested rights, sequestration of rents, oppressive taxation, unequal laws, etc. To the influence of gentlemen of this class the late slave law owes its passage.

"And is it indeed believed that the rights of the rich will be protected by familiarizing the populace with the practice of injustice and cruelty towards the poor? Will the sight of innocent men seized in our streets and sent in fetters to till the broad fields of great landowners increase the reverence felt for land titles? Is it wise to give the people practical lessons in the demolition of all the barriers raised by the common law for the protection of the weak against the strong? Is it true conservatism to obliterate in the masses the sense of justice, the feelings of humanity, the distinction between right and wrong?"

The tacit support given to slavery by the Episcopal Church at large and the active support given to it by many individual clergymen was a source of constant grief to Judge Jay and a frequent subject of his thoughts. "You well know," he wrote to Joseph Sturge, "what a mighty effort has been made by our Northern traders in Southern votes and merchandise, under the leadership of Daniel Webster, to roll back the antislavery tide. To a certain extent they have succeeded. The commercial interest in the great towns, through a rivalry for the Southern trade, has professed great alacrity in slave-catching, and political aspirants for office under the Federal Government find it expedient to make slave-hunting the test of patriotism. But the religious feeling of the commonalty—that is, of those who are not pre-eminently gentlemen of property and standing—is shocked by the enormous cruelty and injustice of the fugitive law. To overcome this feeling, which in its demonstrations is exceedingly inconvenient to our merchants and office-seekers, the clergy have been urged by the press and other agencies to come out in support of the law —in other words, to give the sanction of the gospel of Christ to the enslavement of innocent men. Some pastors who preach in fine churches to rich and fashionable city congregations have complied. You must understand that many of our brokers, merchants, lawyers, and editors were exceedingly scandalized by the opposition of religious people to this vile law, and they have trembled for the honour of our holy religion when some of its professors contended that an impious law was not binding on the conscience."

The position of the church was strongly stated by Jay in a letter to Rev. Hiram Jelliff: "It is one of the most melancholy circumstances of the condition of the coloured people that so many of the ministers of the Lord Jesus Christ are among their most influential enemies. The church of the living God is the great buttress of slavery and caste in the United States. If any plea can be urged in behalf of infidelity, it is that Christianity as represented by multitudes of its official teachers authorizes the abrogation of all its precepts of humility, justice, and benevolence in the treatment of persons to whom God has given a coloured skin. Look at the conventions of

New York and Pennsylvania excluding ministers and disciples of the crucified Redeemer merely because they are poor and despised! I confess, my dear sir, that were I a young man, with no early religious impressions and about to decide on the truth or falsehood of revelation, I fear I should be strongly tempted to believe that a religion such as it is practically exhibited by your cotton-parsons could not and did not proceed from a just and benevolent being. I have had great opportunities of knowing the effect produced by the countenance given to slavery and caste by the church on the faith of many kind-hearted and conscientious people, and in all sincerity I declare that our pro-slavery clergy, our negro-hating clergy, our slave-catching clergy, are the most successful apostles of infidelity in the country. I write thus freely to you because your course is in direct opposition to those I condemn. The Saviour eat, drank, and lodged with the Samaritans, who were the negroes of Judea, a despised, degraded caste, from whom a Jew disdained to receive even a cup of water. . . . May God bless and reward your labours."

Occupying, as Judge Jay did, a position of leadership in both the Episcopal Church and the antislavery movement, it was to him that men most frequently turned for advice on subjects relating to the connection between the church and slavery. From mature minds, such as that of Senator Salmon P. Chase, from divinity students and young men contemplating connection with a religious body, came inquiries regarding the duty of joining the church or of remaining a member. To a young man Jay wrote in 1854: "I shall say nothing of the claims of the Episcopal Church as arising from her doctrines, forms, and government, except that I know of no church which, judged *by its authorized standards*, is more scriptural and more conducive to holiness in this life and to salvation in the next. You desire to enter this church but have not been able to overcome the objection arising from its connection with slavery, and would like to know, for your information, how I reconcile my continuance in this church with my antislavery opinions. Assuredly I could not belong to a church which exacted of its members an admission of the lawfulness of human bondage. Of such a sin and folly the Episcopal Church is guiltless. No sanction of slavery can be found in any of her standards, and hence I can very consistently hold the doctrines of the church and join in its prayers and rites and at the same time regard American slavery as the sum of all villainies. There are in the church slaveholding bishops, clergymen, and communicants, *plenty of them*. But I am not responsible for their presence. . . . There never has been, and I suppose there never will be, a widely extended church without unworthy pastors and members. A *pure* church composed of fallible and sinful men is a figment of the imagination. . . . Many popish doctrines and practices are occasionally advocated by our Puseyites. But I, as a private member of the church, am in no degree responsible for the heresies of Puseyism nor the more disgusting heresies of cotton-divinity. . . . In my opinion, in nine cases out of ten an antislavery Christian can do more good to his own soul, to the cause of Christ, and to the interests of the slave by remaining in his church and there battling for truth and justice, than by going in search of a pure church. It often happens when an abolitionist abandons an alleged pro-slavery church he finds no other that suits him. Hence the public worship of God and the Sacraments are neglected. Gradually he and his family learn to live without God in the world, and finally enter upon that broad road which leads to destruction."

The position assumed by the Episcopal Church towards the rights and elevation of the blacks was indicated by the refusal of the Diocesan Council of New York to admit the coloured church of St. Philip, although the parish was constitutionally entitled to be represented and her minister and delegates were entitled to seats and votes. Judge Jay opposed earnestly a majority report from a committee on the question of their admission, which contended that the applicants belonged to a race "socially degraded, and improper associates for the class of persons who attend our conventions." Such an apology for the violation of the constitutional rights ordained by the State, and such a presentation of the theological views entertained by the committee on the unity of the church and the catholic brotherhood of its members, was not calculated to strengthen the opposition to St. Philip's; and the Christian world breathed more freely when, after a nine years' struggle to obtain a vote on the question maintained by Judge Jay and his son, the coloured parish was admitted by a large majority of both orders.

In 1854 Southern aggression had nearly reached its culminating point. The Missouri Compromise was abrogated; the Kansas-Nebraska Bill threw open to slavery an immense territory hitherto free, under the subterfuge invented by General Cass and Senator Douglas of "popular sovereignty." Slavery was thus to extend over the vast regions in the centre of the continent. An indefinite number of new slave States were to be admitted into the Union, which would give the control of the Senate, and consequently of all legislation, forever to the Slave Power.

In February, 1854, Judge Jay received an invitation to address the Anti-Nebraska Convention of the Free Democracy of Massachusetts. His age and health prevented a journey to Boston, but he wrote to the committee of invitation as follows:

"It is meet and right that the stupendous iniquity now about to be perpetrated should be resisted by the true-hearted citizens of that State which, more than any other in the confederacy, has debauched the moral sentiment of the nation and prepared the community for submission to the most insolent usurpation yet attempted by the Slave Power. The present effort to extend the dominion of the whip to the northern limits of the United States is the legitimate consequence of the disastrous and disgraceful concessions of 1850. Those concessions were effected more through the ability and labours of the late distinguished senator from Massachusetts than of any of his coadjutors. Mr. Webster, avowing the entire constitutionality of the Wilmot Proviso and having voted for it in relation to Oregon, objected to its application to the newly conquered territories on the ground that their *Asiatic scenery* and *geographical conformation* rendered it *physically impossible* for negro slavery ever to exist in them. Unhappily for his novel and extraordinary theory, numerous slaves were at the time he spoke held in California. . . . Slaves are at this day held in New Mexico.

"Mr. Webster, in giving his earnest and cordial support to the atrocious Fugitive-Slave Act, candidly acknowledged on the floor of the Senate that in 'his judgment' Congress had no constitutional power to legislate on the subject, the obligation of surrendering fugitives resting on the States. Yet he scrupled not in his subsequent addresses to speak in terms of unmeasured obloquy of every lawyer who presumed to deny the constitutionality of that horrible law. He admitted the right of Congress to grant the fugitive a trial by jury, yet was unwearied in his advocacy of a law denying to the most helpless of mortals that important safeguard of personal liberty. . . .

"The course of this gentleman at a moment when the dearest principles of liberty, justice, and humanity were vehemently assailed was rapturously applauded by the monied, the literary, and the ecclesiastical aristocracy of Massachusetts, and the New England Church has to a great extent canonized his memory.

"The ardour evinced by the city of Boston in the surrender of Simms, and the intense servility and degradation accompanying that surrender, together with the emphatic endorsement of Mr. Webster's conduct, have exerted an influence in behalf of human bondage and in derogation of Christian obligation far beyond the bounds of Massachusetts. The moral bulwark raised at the North against slavery in times past by the religious sentiment and the respect for the rights of man is nearly demolished.

"The Slave Power, taking advantage of the present paralysis of the Northern conscience and the frantic cupidity of our demagogues and merchants for Southern votes and Southern trade, is about placing its yoke on willing and bending necks.

"Think not that Nebraska is to be the terminus of slaveholding encroachments. New slave States are from time to time to be carved out of Mexico. Cuba is to be wrested from Spain and St. Domingo re-enslaved and annexed. As the field for slave labour widens and widens, the supply will be found inadequate to the demand. The discovery will then be made that both religion and policy require the repeal of the prohibition of the African slave-trade. We shall be told of the Christian duty of bringing the pagans of Africa to our own civilized shores and of preparing them for heaven by the discipline of the whip and the teachings of slave-drivers, while politicans and political economists will insist on the removal of the restriction as essential to the development of our national wealth and enterprise. In vain will Virginia and the other breeding States strive to retain their present lucrative monopoly of the human shambles. The cotton and sugar States, together with the newly acquired slave States, aided by Northern politicians, will establish free trade in the bodies and souls of men.

"The Southern Church is almost without exception the unblushing champion of slavery, while the Northern Church, adopting a time-serving, heartless, and often hypocritical neutrality, and holding in its fraternal embrace slave breeders and slave-traders, has virtually taught that the vilest outrages on both the civil and religious rights of the black man are perfectly compatible with the highest sanctity in his white oppressor. Some of our religious journals are sadly grieved and scandalized by the alleged discovery that certain opponents of slavery are infidels. For my own part, I know of no form of infidelity so hideous as that which impiously claims the authority of Almighty God for abrogating all His laws in behalf of justice and mercy in reference to our conduct towards millions of our countrymen not of the same colour as ourselves. This cutaneous Christianity, so insulting to the Deity, so disastrous to man, is fast becoming the national religion.

"The present crisis is indeed an awful one. While various causes have aided in producing it, its immediate origin is to be traced to the lamentable defection, in 1850, of so many of the rich and influential from truth and justice, liberty and humanity, under the fallacious plea of saving the Union. Well may the Free Democracy of Massachusetts, with their hands and consciences undefiled by oblations on the altar of the American Moloch, now strive to avert the calamity impending over the country. May a long-suffering God bless their efforts and rescue a guilty nation from the punishment it seems anxious to inflict upon itself."

"As to the wickedness of the whole Kansas business," Jay wrote to Charles Sumner, in March, 1856, "I most fully agree with you, and I do not wonder that amid such abounding iniquity you are at a loss what atrocity to assail first. I am very much inclined to look upon every Northern member of Congress who voted for the repeal of the Missouri Compromise as a rascal. This may seem harsh—it is certainly not polite—and yet I am utterly unable to assign a good, honest, religious motive for the vote, or to reconcile it with the fear of God or with love to man. . . . Let us fight on, with all our heart and mind and soul. God is with us, approves our efforts, and whether He shall crown them with success or not, He will not forget our work of faith and labour of love. I have full faith in an ultimate triumph, although you and I may not live to enjoy it. My belief is, that as soon as the North ceases to tremble before the slave-drivers, the non-slaveholders of the South will proclaim their independence and insist upon free speech and a free press, and as soon as these are obtained the doom of slavery is sealed."

The repeal of the Missouri Compromise was the beginning of the end, the fatal step of the South on its road to destruction. Throughout the North the conviction grew that Union and slavery could not exist much longer together. On the 4th of July, 1854, Garrison publicly burned a copy of the Constitution of the United States with the words, " The Union must be dissolved ! " He represented only an extreme sentiment. But the people at large began to calculate the value of this Union for which so many sacrifices had been made. Slavery became odious to many persons hitherto indifferent to the subject, on the ground that it persistently and selfishly placed the Union in peril.

In the summer of 1857 Judge Jay received a circular calling for a National Disunion Convention, to be held at Worcester, signed by T. W. Higginson, Wendell Phillips, Daniel Mann, and W. L. Garrison. To this circular he replied at length, giving his views on the question of separation as it then appeared to him.

"The subject you propose for consideration," he said, "has long been to me one of deep and painful interest. Although fully conscious of the many social, commercial, and political advantages derived from the Federal Union, I am nevertheless convinced that it is at present a most grievous moral curse to the American people. To the people of the South it is a curse by fostering and strengthening and perpetuating an iniquitous, corrupting institution. To the millions of African descent among us it is a curse by riveting the chains of the bondman and deepening the degradation of the free man. To the people of the free States it is a curse by tempting them to trample under foot the obligations of truth, justice, and humanity for the wages of iniquity with which the Federal Government has so abundantly rewarded apostates from liberty and righteousness.

"In my opinion, while the Union continues to be thus a curse it will be indissoluble; if it ever ceases to be a curse, it will be converted into a blessing.

. . . .

"What possible reason have you to expect that those in church and state who have surrendered their consciences to the seductions of the Union will listen to your call and aid you in breaking a power which they glory in saving? While I believe you are doomed to disappointment, I nevertheless rejoice in every exposure of the demoralizing influence of the Union. I rejoice in such exposure, not as tending to bring about dissolution, but to render it unnecessary. When the people of the North cease to idolize the Union, they will cease to offer on its altar their rights and their duties. When released from their thraldom to the Slave Power, they will cease to place its minions in office. When no longer covetous of the votes and the trade of the South, they will no longer be bullied into all manner of wretchedness and all manner of insult by the idea and ever-repeated threats of dissolution. But when this happy time arrives, the Union will be converted from a curse into a blessing. Our divines, instead of vindicating cruelty and oppression, and denouncing as fanatics those who consider the will of God a higher law than an accursed act of Congress, will become preachers of righteousness. Democrats, seeing the Federal patronage wielded by the opponents of slavery, will, in the rapidity and extent of their conversion to truth and justice, eclipse all the marvels of New England revivals; and men who for years have been bowed to the earth by spinal weakness will as by miracle stand erect. When all this happens, the North will continue its Union with the South; and you yourselves will have no wish to see that Union severed.

"At the close of the war, Washington, solicitous that the divine favour might rest on the new-born nation, publicly offered the prayer that God would dispose us all to do justice and love mercy. May the Union, when exerting an influence in accordance with this prayer, be indissoluble; but may God forbid that it may ever be saved by promoting, extending, and perpetuating injustice and cruelty, by invoking the wrath of Heaven, and becoming a proverb and a reproach among the nations of the earth."

CHAPTER VIII.

DEATH OF JUDGE JAY.—HIS POSITION AMONG ANTISLAVERY MEN.—HIS OTHER PUBLIC AND PHILANTHROPIC INTERESTS.—HIS PRIVATE LIFE.—HIS CHARACTER.

JUDGE JAY was not destined to live to see the triumph of the antislavery cause and of the constitutional principles to which he had devoted his life. Several years of failing health preceded his death, which took place at Bedford, October the 14th, 1858.

His career in the antislavery cause, dating from the Missouri Compromise in 1821, was in several respects unique, and among the leaders of the movement his position continued to be distinctive.

His first active efforts in favour of the slave, the presentation to Congress in 1826 of petitions for the abolition of slavery in the District of Columbia, were marked by a careful regard to the provisions of the United States Constitution. At the first formation of antislavery societies he feared that philanthropic enthusiasm might place the movement in a wrong position by a failure to recognize those provisions. His advice was asked by the men who organized the American Society in Philadelphia, and it was carried into effect by the insertion into the constitution of the society of a complete recognition of the supreme national law, in strict accordance with which, only, the objects of the society should be sought. To maintain the abolitionists in the impregnable position thus adopted was the constant and characteristic labour of Jay's life. This position, consistently held by him against unconstitutional doctrines advanced by both abolitionists and slaveholders, was the position adopted by the Republican party in 1854, and maintained until real union and real liberty were won together.

The antislavery movement was begun and supported by those whom Lincoln called "the plain people." Men of "property and standing" were generally passively if not actively hostile. It received little help from the churches, from the learned professions or the wealthy mercantile classes. It was a very unpopular cause, denounced by politicians, merchants, and lawyers, despised by many of the clergy, certain to bring social and business injury, if not active persecution, to whomsoever adopted it. Hence the championship of William Jay derived a special importance. His judicial and social position, his independent means, his active membership in the most aristocratic of churches, made him a leader of peculiar value. His advocacy of the cause could be attributed neither to ignorant fanaticism nor to disorganizing tendencies. He set an example to the class most able and least willing to oppose the curse of slavery.

A third peculiarity of Jay's position among antislavery men was the nature of the work which he performed. Without health sufficient to make long journeys at a time when travelling was difficult, seldom leaving his country home, he was rarely seen at the meetings and conventions of the abolitionists. He was a voice, speaking words of reason, moderation and authority in times of blind excitement; a voice which spoke at the right moment and was always heard with respect. Jay's activity lay in his pen. In a crisis when the judicious course of action or the accurate view of events was obscured by doubt and passion, a pamphlet or a public letter from Judge Jay cast a clear and steady light. His writings were consulted by the most eminent men when considering subjects connected with slavery. Of this a notable instance was the use made of Jay's argument on the "Amistad" case by John Quincy Adams when addressing the House of Representatives in that celebrated cause. These writings form a continuous and lucid commentary on the history of the long and varied struggle between the forces of slavery and of freedom.

The published works of Judge Jay present but a part of the fruits and the influence of his pen. His correspondence was voluminous and extended to the rank and file as well as to the leaders of the anti-slavery movement. Constant resort was made to him for information and advice, which was always given with frankness and care.*

---

* Among those with whom Judge Jay was most often in communication may be mentioned: Arthur and Lewis Tappan, Rev. S. S. Jocelyn,

We may close appropriately our review of Jay's antislavery work with remarks made after his death to the coloured people of New York by Frederick Douglass, who escaped from the slave-driver to urge with native eloquence the emancipation of his race: " In common with you, my friends, I wear the hated complexion which William Jay never hated. I have worn the galling chain which William Jay earnestly endeavoured to break. I have felt the heavy lash, and have experienced in my own person the cruel wrongs which caused his manly heart to melt in pity for the slave. . . . In view of the mighty struggle for freedom in which we are now engaged, and the tremendous odds arrayed against us, every coloured man and every friend of the coloured man in this country must deeply feel the great loss we have sustained in this death, and look around with anxious solicitude for the man who shall rise to fill the place now made vacant. With emphasis it may be said of him, he was our wise counsellor, our firm friend, and our liberal benefactor. Against the fierce onsets of popular abuse he was our shield; against governmental intrigue and oppression he was our learned, able,

---

Rev. A. A. Phelps, Robert Vaux, E. Wright, Jr., Joshua Leavitt, Samuel J. May, Reuben Crandall, James G. Birney, Theodore Sedgwick, Beriah Green, Gerrit Smith, John Scoble of England, Mrs. L. M. Child, Miss Grimke, Wm. Goodell, G. Bailey, Jr., Rev. Dr. Morrison of England, Gov. R. W. Habersham, W. W. Anderson of Jamaica, W. I., Joseph Sturge of England, Jabez D. Hammond, Geo. W. Alexander of England, William Slade, John Quincy Adams, Wm. H. Seward, S. P. Chase, Prof. C. D. Cleveland, Thomas Clarkson of England, Sir W. Colebrook, governor of New Brunswick, Charles Sumner, Chief-Justice Hornblower, J. G. Palfrey, and John P. Hale.

and faithful defender; against the crafty counsels of wickedness in high places, where mischief is framed by law and sin is sanctioned and supported by religion, he was a perpetual and burning rebuke."

Besides his work for the negro race, William Jay had various public and philanthropic interests. Prominent among these were the duties of judge of Westchester County, which he exercised for more than twenty-five years. Jay revised the rules of the court, which had been handed down almost unchanged since 1728; and he introduced a strict observance of forms, which, combined with his prompt and explicit decisions, made the Westchester court one of the most dignified in the country. The sittings were held alternately at White Plains and at Bedford, the half-shire towns of the county. Jay also attended to chamber business in other towns. At that period the Westchester bar embraced many lawyers of marked ability, such as R. R. Voorhis, Aaron Ward, William Nelson, Peter Jay Munro, J. W. Strong, Minot Mitchell, and James Smith; and from New York, Alexander McDonald, William M. Price, and Peter Augustus Jay frequently appeared among them. It has been said of Judge Jay's charges to grand juries that "they commanded attention, from their clear exposition of the law without the slightest concession to the popular currents of the day and with careful regard to constitutional rights, morality, and justice." These charges were frequently requested for publication as timely reminders of legal and moral truths, the relation of which to current events was being overlooked. Judge Jay's conduct on the bench caused his reappointment term after term by governors of opposing political parties; and after his death, when a pro-slavery faction endeavoured to remove his portrait from the court-house at White Plains, members of the bar who disagreed with Jay's abolition opinions were foremost in preventing any act of disrespect to his memory.

Jay's philanthropy was religious in its motive and practical in its activity. A life-long worker in the cause of temperance, his efforts produced substantial results, as in the legislation proposed by him which forbade the sale of intoxicating liquors on credit.

For many years a member and president of the Peace Society, he was not satisfied with exposing the evils of war. His mind sought and found a remedy for it in the system of international arbitration, of which the practicability was immediately acknowledged, and towards which the civilized world has since turned with constantly growing confidence.

The organization of the American Bible Society in the face of the opposition of the authorities in his own church displayed in Jay's early life the self-reliance and independence of character which gave so much strength to his later career. Always true to his church, he never compromised his convictions to fit a position in which that church was untrue to itself. During the antislavery movement the churches were hostile. Fearful of alienating their Southern members and the Northern men whose business interests demanded subserviency to the Slave Power, hardly any ecclesiastical organization was guiltless of lending a passive support to slavery. Theological students, on leaving their seminary, were cautioned by their instructors to avoid the troublesome topic if they would be successful ministers of Christ. Clergymen who preached that property in man was sinful were disciplined by ecclesiastical superiors or cast off by outraged Christian congregations. An orthodox religious newspaper was the safest printed matter for a Northern man to have in his possession when travelling in the South. The Episcopal Church had its slaveholding bishops and ministers, not a few of whom justified slavery from the Scriptures. It had in the North its "cotton divines," who enjoined from the pulpit obedience to the odious law which sought to make slave-catchers of Christian men and women. It went so far as persistently to infringe its own laws by shutting the doors of its conventions upon legally chosen delegates of congregations composed of free coloured men. The church of Christ was turned into a social club which did not hesitate to exclude a black man as an "unfit associate." Shocked at this attitude, many conscientious men withdrew from the communion. But such a course was inconsistent with Jay's character. False and repulsive as was to him such a conception of the Christian religion, he refused, as a churchman, to accept it. He remained in the ranks, striving by his own conduct to show that a man could be a good churchman and hate slavery at the same time. Fearless in his expression of Christian truth, he was for twenty years a thorn in the side of pro-slavery churchmen, and a rallying-point for those who understood better the spirit of Christianity and recognized the brotherhood of man before God.

Jay's private life was happy and peaceful. The library at Bedford, with its book-shelves crowded to the ceiling and its windows looking out over the hills of Westchester to the blue outlines of the Catskills, claimed a considerable portion of every day. The hours there passed in reflection and in literary labour were hours of pleasure, enhanced by the desire and the hope of usefulness.

Out-of-doors were the avocations of a country life, which Jay was well constituted to enjoy: the farm, with its interesting record of crops and growing livestock; the garden, where a great variety of flowers and vegetables flourished within hedges of old box; the lawn, with its trees planted by his father and himself—all these gave occupation in pleasing contrast to that of the library. The public roads in the neighbourhood of the Jay farm are now adorned and shaded by noble trees planted by the Judge. Along these roads and over the Westchester hills he loved to ride on horseback, an exercise and pleasure which he enjoyed until the last year of his life. Judge Jay preferred to consider Bedford as a farm rather than as a country seat, and he observed to Bishop Coxe in this regard that a farm without a gate or a fence out of repair was more to his taste than an ornamental estate. The weak eyesight and somewhat delicate health which in his youth seemed a misfortune as debarring him from a career of activity in the city turned in the end to his advantage. A happier life than that at Bedford could hardly have been devised for him; and it is probable that the studious retirement of his country library gave to his views on public questions a thoroughness and moderation greater than could have been attained amidst the hurry and distraction of a great city.

In his family relations, Jay was still more fortunate. His wife lived to be his sympathetic companion until 1856, when he himself was near his end. Her accomplishments, especially in reading and drawing, her grace, gentleness, and goodness, her natural charity, added immeasurably to the happiness of Jay's life. "I have always regarded her," said the late Rev. J. W. Alexander, "as one of the happiest specimens of a Christian lady that it has been my lot to meet. Intelligent, graceful, pious, gentle, sportive in the right place, generous and catholic, she awakened a sincere respect and attachment, and our memory of her is blessed." The late Bishop Horatio Potter of New York, speaking of her later life, said: "The serene composure, the sweet simplicity and dignity, bespoke a peaceful and elevated spirit, and made an impression on the most transient visitor never to be effaced." Dr. John Henry Hobart, son of the Bishop, wrote to John Jay: "Your mother, always gentle, placid, and cheerful, with an unfailing smile and

Augustus Jay

pleasant words for her young guests, sympathizing with their boyish enthusiasm for poetry and romance, and tempering their ardour with counsel and caution, which her own sensitive spirit conveyed in the most delicate forms—of her I must speak thus feelingly; it only indicates the debt of gratitude I owe to her memory."

Judge Jay had one brother, Peter Augustus Jay, who was thirteen years his senior. Between the brothers there continued through life an uninterrupted affection and confidence. Peter Augustus led an active professional and social life in New York City, holding office as judge, as recorder, and as a member of the State Assembly. On his death, in 1843, high tributes to his ability as a jurist and to his character as a public-spirited citizen were paid by Chancellor Kent, Chief-Justice Samuel Jones, and David B. Ogden. As a member of the Assembly, he was conspicuous in the advocacy of various important measures, among which may be mentioned his efforts to extend the right of suffrage to black citizens of the State. Peter Augustus Jay was not himself prominent in the antislavery cause, but he was generally in sympathy with his brother's work.

The Right Reverend A. Cleveland Coxe, Bishop of Western New York, was a frequent visitor in his youth at Bedford. Some extracts from a letter written by him to John Jay afford an interesting view of the domestic life of the Judge's home:

" William Jay was one of those true sons of the

Republic who inherited sound views of its constitutional system from your illustrious grandfather, and from personal acquaintance with some other fathers of the nation who were high in the confidence of Washington and shared his just and lofty ideas of national policy. Your father was one of those born statesmen who breathed under the inspiration of such ideas, and was animated by them to efforts for the preservation of the Constitution itself in degenerate days. Those were the days when the 'spoils-system' had begun to act with corrosive effect on public affairs and public men. The science of true statesmanship seemed ready to perish. The country fell into the hands of mere politicians, with whom legislation was a trade and a struggle for personal aggrandizement. The epoch had little use for men of pure patriotism, but your father, incapable of ambition or the pursuit of personal ends, stood aside and devoted himself with intrepidity to unpopular principles, of which he foresaw the utility, while he was hardly less prophetic of the cruel war which must be the consequence of popular indifference and blindness to the national perils. He was little seen, but greatly felt, and has left a mark on the diplomacy of his time which is a gain to humanity and to civilization.

"I cannot forget the charms of that domestic life which he made so attractive to his children and to the large circle of kindred and friends who were admitted to its enjoyments. It was in 1836 that, with our beloved friend Hobart, I was invited to spend the

Christmas holidays at Bedford. We were boys together at that time, and I remember to what hours we prolonged our recreations, with no other restriction than your father's cheerful injunction, as he bade us good-night: 'Young gentlemen, please remember not to laugh too loudly; it might deprive some of us of the sleep which you seem not to require for yourselves.' How merrily we 'saw the old year out and the new year in,' that Christmas-tide! I often thought of Irving's 'Bracebridge Hall' as realized in America, in the home of your happy boyhood. Year after year, winter and summer, through college life, you led me to renew my holidays in Bedford. How much I learned from your father's condescension to boyhood in conversing with his boy-visitors as if they were men! He drew out our opinions and encouraged us to state them frankly when he suspected that we had the boldness to prefer our crude ideas to his own judicial and grave conceptions of fact and principle. He played chess with his youthful guests, but never permitted them to beat him, as that would have been no compliment to lads who worked hard and wished to win in a fair game.

"I have rarely seen a household in which family life was ordered more particularly with reference to religion. There was much of the Huguenot in the piety of the Judge, but nothing of the Puritan. Family prayers were observed twice a day, the servants attending and sharing in the responses. After evening prayers in those early days, we enjoyed a few cotillons and contra-dances, Mrs. Jay presiding at the piano. And when the ladies had withdrawn, chess-playing and other games occupied us, not infrequently until after midnight. Sundays in the old homestead, after church-going, were like other days, save in the chastened cheerfulness of conversation and employment. A feature of Sunday evenings was the custom for every member of the family to recite something in prose or poetry, and the Judge often closed such recitals by reading selections from Bishop Heber, Mr. Milman, and other favourites of those times. In the third decade of this century, the daughters of 'the governor,' Mrs. Banyer and Miss Jay, were often the guests of their brother. They would have been interesting figures in any society, and were eminent in New York for their Christian virtues and devotion to every good work. The elder sister, born in Spain, seemed to preserve in her face and carriage something borrowed from her native climate, while Mrs. Banyer, born in France, was not less conspicuously marked by characteristics of her French ancestry. While the only son of Judge Jay is a recognized type of his father's principles and character, his daughters not less resembled their mother—a lady whose memory I hold in very great respect, with an affectionate estimate of her worth as a beautiful example of her gracious sex, in all characteristics 'wherein there is virtue and wherein there is praise.'

"I feel, at this distance of time, that I owe much to

the friendship of Judge Jay, apart from the pleasures it conferred upon me. How much he taught me! How often his maxims led me to correct my faults, though he never seemed to instruct, much less to rebuke! Even in his decline, and when he was nearing the end, he favoured me with an occasional letter. Need I say that, while entirely free from cant and pharisaic professions, such letters were models of Christian submission, and not less of 'faith, hope, and charity'? I have frequently reflected upon them as I find myself approaching the end. His lofty example leads me to say with the inspired moralist: 'Mark the perfect man and behold the upright, for the end of that man is peace.'"

BIBLIOGRAPHY.

THE LIFE OF JOHN JAY. With Selections from his Correspondence and Miscellaneous Papers. In two volumes, 1833.

WAR AND PEACE. The Evils of the First and a Plan for Preserving the Last. London, 1842.

A REVIEW OF THE CAUSES AND CONSEQUENCES OF THE MEXICAN WAR, 1849.

MISCELLANEOUS WRITINGS ON SLAVERY, 1853. In which are collected:

Inquiry into the Character and Tendency of the American Colonization, and American Antislavery Societies.

A View of the Action of the Federal Government in Behalf of Slavery.

On the Condition of the Free People of Colour in the United States.

Address to the Friends of Constitutional Liberty, on the Violation by the United States House of Representatives of the Right of Petition.

Introductory Remarks to the Reproof of the American Church contained in the recent "History of the Protestant Episcopal Church in America" by the Bishop of Oxford.

A Letter to the Right Reverend L. Silliman Ives, Bishop of the Protestant Church in the State of North Carolina.

Address to the Inhabitants of New Mexico and California, on the Omission by Congress to provide them with Territorial Governments, and on the Social and Political Evils of Slavery.

Letter to Hon. William Nelson, M. C., on Mr. Clay's Compromise.

A Letter to the Hon. Samuel A. Eliot, Representative in Congress from the City of Boston, in Reply to his Apology for voting for the Fugitive-Slave Bill.

An Address to the Antislavery Christians of the United States. Signed by a number of clergymen and others.

Letter to Rev. R. S. Cook, Corresponding Secretary of the American Tract Society.

Letter to Lewis Tappan, Esq., Treasurer of the American Missionary Society.

PAMPHLETS.

Report of the Bedford Society for the Suppression of Vice, 1815.

Letter to Venders of Ardent Spirits, 1815.

Answer to Bishop Hobart's Pastoral Letter on the Subject of Bible Societies, by an Episcopalian, 1815.

Memoir on the Subject of a General Bible Society, by a Citizen of New York, 1816.

Appeal in Behalf of the American Bible Society, by a Lay Member of the Convention, 1816.

Dialogue between a Clergyman and a Layman on the Subject of Bible Societies, by a Churchman, 1817.

Remarks on a Petition to the Legislature praying for the Repeal of the Acts for Improving the Agriculture of this State, by a Westchester Farmer, 1821.

Letter to Bishop Hobart occasioned by the Strictures on Bible Societies contained in his late Charge to the Convention of New York, by a Churchman, 1823.

Letter to Bishop Hobart in Reply to the Pamphlet addressed by him to the Author under the Signature of "Corrector," by William Jay, 1823.

Reply to a Second Letter to the Author from Bishop Hobart, with Remarks on his Hostility to Bible Societies, by William Jay, 1823.

Essay on the Importance of the Sabbath considered merely as a Civil Institution, 1826.

Essay on the Perpetuity and Divine Authority of the Sabbath. Published by the Synod of Albany, 1827.

Remarks on the Proposed Changes in the Liturgy and Confirmation Service, 1827.

The Office of Assistant Bishop inconsistent with the Constitution of the Protestant Episcopal Church, 1829.

Essay on Duelling, 1830.

Address to the Inhabitants of Westchester County on Temperance, 1834.

Addresses to the Westchester County Auxiliary Bible Society, 1836, 1839, 1841, 1845, and other years.

Address before the New York Female Bible Society, 1840.

Letter of Hon. William Jay to Hon. Theodore Frelinghuysen on Slavery, 1844.

Address before the American Peace Society, 1845.

Trial by Jury in New York, 1846.

Address to the Non-Slaveholders of the South, on the Social and Political Evils of Slavery, 1849.

The Calvary Pastoral, with Comments, a Tract for the Times, 1849.

Reply to Mr. Webster's 7th of March Speech, 1850.

Reply to Remarks of the Rev. Moses Stuart in his pamphlet entitled "Conscience and the Constitution." J. A. Gray, New York, 1850.

The Kossuth Excitement, 1852.

The Bible against Slavery. J. K. Wellman, Adrian, Michigan, 1852.

Petition of the American Peace Society to the United States Senate in behalf of Stipulated Arbitration, 1853.

An Examination of the Mosaic Law of Servitude, "The Statutes of the Lord are right — Psalm xix. 8." M. W. Dodd, New York, 1854.

"The Eastern War," an Argument for the Cause of Peace. Address before the American Peace Society, 1855.

A Letter to the Rev. Wm. Berrian, D.D., on the Resources, Present Position, and Duties, of Trinity Church, occasioned by his late Pamphlet, "Facts against Fancy." A. D. Randolph & Co., New York.

Judge Jay left in Manuscript an elaborate Commentary, the work of many years, on the Old and New Testaments.

INDEX.

Abolition Intelligencer, the, 28.
Abolition movement, its early history, 18 *et seq.*
Abolition societies, early, 23, 27.
Abolitionists, hatred of, 41, 42, 56, 67, 135, 136.
———, differences among, 83, 103.
Adams, Charles Francis, 129.
———, John Quincy, 25, 31, 158, 159.
Alexander, George W., 159.
———, J. W., 164.
American and Foreign Antislavery Society, formation of, 103.
American Antislavery Society, formation of, 49, 50; division in, 103.
Anderson, W. W., 159.
Anti-Annexation Meeting, in New York, 126.
Antislavery movement, development of, 39 *et seq.*
Antislavery societies, formation of, 45.
Antislavery Society of New York City, 46, 47.
Aspinwall, John, 12.

Bailey, G., Jr., xvii, 159.
Banyer, Mrs., 125, 167.
Bedford, 8, 9, 163.
Benezet, Anthony, 19.
Benson, Judge, 38.
Bible Society, iii, 10, 11, 12.
Birney, James G., xvi, 63, 103, 107, 117, 118, 159.
Bogardus, General, 46.
Bolton, John, 12.
Bouck, Gov., 14, 124, 125.
Boudinot, Elias, iii, 11, 12, 28.
Bourgueny, Baron, vi.
Bradish, Luther, 110.
Brent, W. L., 35.
Broglie, Duc de, 63, 126.
Brown, David P., 54.

Brownson, Dr. Orestes A., xix.
Brune, Baron, vi.
Buol-Schauenstein, Count, vi.
Buren, Van, Martin, 107, 124.
Burling, William, 18.

Calhoun, John C., xii, 4.
Canterbury, persecution at, 42.
Cass, Lewis, 149.
Cavour, Count, vi, xviii.
Chambers, John, 9.
Channing, W. E., 56.
Chapman, Mrs., xvi, 91.
Chase, Salmon P., 146, 159.
Chatham Street Chapel, 47, 53.
Child, Mrs. Lydia Maria, xvii, 40, 67, 112, 159.
Circourt, M. de, v.
Clarendon, Lord, vi, 131.
Clarkson, Matthew, 12.
Clarkson, Thomas, 159.
Clay, Henry, 24, 32.
Cleveland, C. D., 159.
Clinton, De Witt, 12, 14, 31, 32.
Clinton Hall, 46.
Cobden, R., vi.
Colebrook, Sir W., 159.
Colonization Society, 26.
Commercial Advertiser, 55.
Compromise of 1850, 137.
Constitutional questions, xi, 86, 87, 89, 91, 99.
Cooper, J. Fenimore, 2, 3, 5, 9, 14.
Cornish, Samuel E., 73.
Cortlandt, Van, Eve, 9.
———, Jacobus, 9.
———, Mary, 9.
———, Pierre, 9.
Cotton-gin, the, 23.
Courier and Inquirer, 47, 55.
Cowley, Lord, vi.
Cox, Abraham L., 55, 73.
Cox, Samuel H., 64.
Coxe, A. Cleveland, 165.
Crandall, Miss, 42.
———, Reuben, 41, 159.
Cummings, John, 13.

INDEX. 177

Dane, Nathan, 20.
Davis, Henry, 3.
———, Jefferson, xii.
Delavan, Edward, 61.
Denison, Charles W., 103.
Derby, Lord, vii.
Disunion, 153, 154, 155.
Douglas, Senator, 149.
Douglass, Frederick, 159.
Duelling, essay on, 13.
Dwight, Timothy, 7.

Earle, Thomas, 107.
Edwards, Jonathan, 23.
Ellison, Thomas, 1.
Emancipation, gradual, 41.
———, immediate, 23, 40, 41, 43.
———, in West Indies, 45.
Emancipator, the, 28, 75.
Episcopal Church, its attitude towards slavery, 132, 133, 144, 145, 147.
Evarts, Jeremiah, 12.
Everett, Alexander H., 82.

Fitzmaurice, Lord Edmond, v.
Forsythe, John, 35.
Franklin, Benjamin, iv, 23.
Frelinghuysen, Theodore, 48.
Frere, John Hookham, 126.
Fugitive-Slave Law, 140, 141, 142, 143, 144.

Gadsden, Christopher Edward, 4.
Gallatin, Albert, 127.
Gallaudet, Thomas H., 4.
Garrison, William L., xvii, 40, 51, 53, 63, 64, 77, 84, 86, 89, 102, 153, 154.
Gay, S. H., xvii.
Gayle, Gov., 74.
Genius of Universal Emancipation, 28.
Gibbons, James S., xvii.
Giddings, Joshua R., 129.
Gladstone, W. E., vi.
Goodell, William, xvii, 27, 40, 107, 159.
Gouverneur, Samuel L., 65.
Gray, William, 12.
Grayson, William, 20.
Green, Rev. Beriah, 60, 159.

Green, Oliver, 30.
Griffin, George, 12.
Grimke, Misses, xvii, 91, 159.
———, Thomas Smith, 4.
Grundy, Felix, 12.

Habersham, R. W., 13, 159.
Hale, John P., 159.
Hamilton, Alexander, 23.
———, James, 35.
Hammond, J. D., 159.
Harrison, W. H., 107.
Henry, John B., 8.
———, Patrick, 20, 21.
Hicks, Elias, 27.
Higginson, T. W., 154.
Hillhouse, James A., 4.
Hobart, Bishop, iv, 11, 13.
———, John Henry, 164.
Holley, Myron, 107.
Holly, Horace, 6.
Hopkins, Samuel, 19, 23.
Hopper, Isaac T., xvii.
Hornblower, Chief-Justice, 159.
Horton, Gilbert, case of, 29, 30, 31.
Hubner, Baron, vi.
Huntington, William, 4.

Immediate Emancipation, first proclaimed as a duty, 23.
International arbitration, v, 130, 131.
Ives, Bishop, x.

Jackson, Andrew, 77.
———, Francis, 102.
———, J. C., 103.
Jarvis, Samuel F., 4.
Jay, John, iv, 1, 5, 9, 12, 20, 23, 38, 39, 127.
———, John, 2d, 55.
———, Miss, 125, 167.
———, Peter Augustus, 160, 165.
——— Treaty, iv.
———, William, his birth, 1; education, 2; at Yale College, 4, 6; studies law, 8; marriage, 8; begins life at Bedford, 8, 9; begins philanthropic work, 10; advocates Bible Societies, 10; conflict with Bishop Hobart and High-Church party, 10, 11, 13; organizes American

Bible Society, 11, 12; takes prize for essay on the Sabbath, 13; for essay on duelling, 13; appointed judge, 14; early adoption of antislavery cause, 28; espouses cause of Gilbert Horton, 29; begins movement for abolition of slavery in District of Columbia, 29, 32, 34, 36, 37; writes "Life of John Jay," 39; his view of slavery problem in 1833, 43, 44; consulted regarding formation of American Antislavery Society, 45; advises acknowledgment of constitutional provisions, 45, 46; invited to join in organizing the American Antislavery Society, 49; his views on such an organization, 50; suggests a definite avowal of constitutional principles, 50, 51; becomes a member of Executive Committee of American Antislavery Society, 57; publishes his "Inquiry," 58; its influence, 60, 61; appointed foreign corresponding secretary, 63; gives advice on right to use the mails, 65; his "Address to the Public," 69; elected president of New York State Antislavery Society, 77; his reply to President Jackson's message, 78; protests against the introduction of irrelevant doctrines into antislavery societies, 84, 86, 100; protests against unconstitutional doctrines, 87, 90; defeats Alvan Stewart's resolution, 93; his opinion of the danger of unconstitutional doctrines, 90, 94; his opinion of Stewart's position, 95; his loss of faith in the usefulness of antislavery societies, 97, 100; placed on Executive Committee of American and Foreign Antislavery Society, 103; resigns membership in American Antislavery Society, 103; views on the woman question, 103, 104; his "View of the Action of the Federal Government," 105; his "Condition of the Free People of Colour," 106; his "Violation of the Right of Petition," 106; his attitude towards Liberty party in 1840, 107, 108, 109; his attitude towards antislavery societies after the schism, 112, 113, 114, 115, 116; his attitude towards Liberty party in 1843, 117, 118, 119, 120, 121; his views on the annexation of Texas, 118, 127, 128; nominated for Senator by the Liberty party, 120; deprived of his seat on the bench, 122; his visit to Europe, 125; his "Review of the Mexican War," 127, 128; his "War and Peace," and plan for international arbitration, 130, 131; his attitude towards the "come-outers," 132; his work in the Episcopal Church in favour of the slave, 132, 133, 144, 145, 147, 162; "Letter to Bishop Ives," 133; reply to Webster, 137, 138; attitude towards the Fugitive-Slave Law, 140, 141, 142, 143; views on the Kansas-Nebraska Bill, 149, 150, 152; views on disunion, 153, 154, 155; his death, 156; his distinctive position among antislavery men, 156, 157, 158; his writings, 158; his conduct as judge, 160; other philanthropic work, 161; his position as a churchman, 161, 162; his life at Bedford, 163, 164; his family life, 164, 165, 166.

———, William, 2d, 5, 8.
———, Mrs. William, 8, 164.

Jefferson, Thomas, 20, 24.
Jelliff, Hiram, 145.
Jocelyn, Simeon S., xvii, 73, 158.
Johnston, Oliver, xvii.
Jones, Samuel, 165.

Katonah, 9.
Keith, George, 18.
Kelley, Miss Abby, 102.
Kendall, Amos, 64, 65.
Kent, James, 53, 61, 127, 165.
King, Rufus, 20.

Langdon, John, 12.
Law, William, 13.
Lay, Benjamin, 18.
Leavitt, Joshua, xvi, 49, 73, 103, 107, 159.
Lee, Richard H., 20.
Leggett, William, 56.
Liberalist, the, 28.
Liberator, the, 40.
Liberty party, 107, 117, 118, 119.
Lincoln, Abraham, xiii, xviii, 157.
Loring, Ellis Gray, xvii, 87, 90, 91.
Lovejoy, Elijah P., 82.
Ludlow, Henry G., 53.
Lundy, Benjamin, 27, 40.
Lyons, Lord, xiv.

McAllister, Matthew H., 13.
McDonald, Alexander, 160.
McDuffie, George, 35.
McVickar, John, 8.
Mails, destruction of, 64.
Malmsbury, Lord, vii, 131.
Mann, Daniel, 154.
Marcy, Governor, 76, 110.
May, Samuel J., 50, 51, 86, 91, 159.
Miner, Charles, 32, 37.
Missouri Compromise, 24.
Mitchell, Minot, 122, 160.
Mobs, 56, 82, 135.
Morris, Thomas, 117.
Morrison, Dr., 159.
Mott, Lucretia, xvii.
Munro, Peter Jay, 160.

Nelson, William, 160.
Noyes Academy, 42.

Ogden, David B., 48, 165.
Orloff Count, vi.
Owen, John, 29.

Palfrey, J. G., 159.
Peyster, de, Frederic, 12.
Phelps, Amos A., 53, 86, 103, 159.
Phillips, Wendell, xvii, 154.
Pickering, Thomas, 20.
Pierpont, John, 4.
Pinckney, Charles C., 12.
Pintard, John, 12.
Playfair, Sir Lyon, viii, 132.
Potter, Alonzo, 61.
———, Horatio, 164.
Purvis, Robert, 53.

Quincy, Edmund, xvii.
Quincy, Josiah, 141.

Rankin, John, 27, 73.
Rensselaer, Van, Stephen, 12.
Reporter, the, 113.
Republican party, 52.
"Review of the Mexican War," ix.
Richard, Henry, vi, 131.
Riots, pro-slavery, 46, 54.
Romeyne, John B., 12.
Rush, Benjamin, 19.
Rutgers, Henry, 12.

St. Clair, Alanson, 91.
St. Philip's Church, 148.
Sandiford, Ralph, 18.
Sandwich, Lord, 19.
Scoble, John, 159.
Sedgwick, Henry D., 37.
———, Susan, 3.
———, Theodore, 127, 159.
———, Mrs. Theodore, 61.
Sewall, Samuel, 18.
Seward, W. H., xiv, 110, 159.

Simms, 150.
Slade, William, 159.
Slave Power, growth of, 135.
Smith, Gerrit, xvi, 77, 83, 103, 107, 118, 141, 159.
———, Goldwin, xviii.
———, James, 160.
———, John Cotton, 12.
Spring, Gardiner, 4.
Stanton, Henry B., 103, 119.
Stephens, A. H., xv.
Stevens, Alexander H., 4.
Stewart, Alvan, 52, 76, 92, 95, 96, 99, 107.
———, Charles, 53.
Stone, James A., 53.
Storrs, Henry R., 4.
Stowe, Harriet B., xvii.
Strong, J. W., 160.
Sturge, Joseph, v, 130, 131, 144, 159.
Stuyvesant, Peter G., 61.
Sumner, Charles, 136, 152, 159.

Tabernacle, the Broadway, 92.
Tappan, Arthur, xvi, 40, 45, 49, 53, 55, 64, 67, 68, 73, 102, 103, 158.
———, Lewis, xvi, 40, 47, 54, 73, 75, 103, 113, 158.
Taylor, Nathaniel W., 4.
Thompson, George, 63, 67.
Tighlman, William, 12.
Tocqueville, de, A., 15.
Tompkins, Daniel D., 12.
Torrey, Charles T., 101.
Tucker, Beverly, xiii.

Utica Convention, 76.

Varick, Richard, 12.
Vaux, Robert, 159.
Vergennes, Count de, v.
Villamarina, Marquis de, vi.
Voorhis, R. R., 160.

Walewski, Count, vi.
Walworth, Chancellor, 48.
"War and Peace," v, 130, 131.
Ward, Aaron, 34, 160.
———, Samuel R., xvii.

Washington, Bushrod, 12.
———, George, 155.
Wayne, James M., 13.
Webster, Daniel, 137, 139, 144, 150.
Weekly Emancipator, 40.
Weld, Theodore D., xvii.
Whittier, John G., xvii, 40, 51, 103.
Wickliffe, Charles A., 35.
Wilberforce, Samuel, 133, 134.
Williams, Ransom G., 74, 75.
Wilson, Henry, 58.
Wirt, William, 12.
Woman question, the, 103, 104, 105.
Woolman, John, 19.
Worthington, Governor, 12.
Wright, Elizur, Jr , xvii, 40, 49, 53, 65, 67, 73, 107, 159.
———, Theodore S., 73.

APPENDIX.

REPRESENTATIVES OF ANTISLAVERY OPINION IN NEW YORK IN 1864.

A COMPLIMENTARY breakfast was given to Professor Goldwin Smith at the rooms of the Union League Club, on Union Square, New York, on Saturday morning, the 12th November, 1864.

The following gentlemen joined in the invitation:

Jonathan Sturges, *President of Union League Club, New York;* Charles Butler; John C. Hamilton; Wm. Curtis Noyes, LL.D.; Hon. Horace Greeley, *Editor of the New York Tribune;* Hon. H. J. Raymond, *Editor of the New York Times;* Rev. H. W. Bellows, D.D., *President of United States Sanitary Commission;* Francis Lieber, LL.D., *Professor of History in Columbia College;* Vincenzo Botta, Ph.D.; Elliot C. Cowdin; Col. James McKaye; Wm. H. Webb; Geo. C. Ward; Isaac Ferris, D.D., *Chancellor of the University;* Wm. Allen Butler; Hon. Samuel B. Ruggles, LL.D.; Hon. Wm. E. Dodge; Wm. H. Osborn; A. Gracie King; C. A. Bristed; Cyrus W. Field; T. B. Coddington; Wm. J. Hoppin; Charles H. Marshall; Alfred Pell; Horace Webster, LL.D., *Principal of the Free Academy;* John Jay; Wm. Cullen Bryant; Wm. M. Evarts; Parke Godwin, *Editor of the Evening Post;* F. A. P. Barnard, LL.D., *President of Columbia College;* W. T. Blodgett; Geo. Griswold; Hon. Chas. P. Kirkland; James Brown; John E. Williams; A. A. Low, *President of the Chamber of Commerce;* John Austin Stevens, Jr., *Secretary of the Chamber of Commerce;* Geo. T. Strong; John C. Green; Richard M. Hunt; Geo. W. Blunt; John A. Weeks; Otis D. Swan; Col. L. G. B. Cannon; Theodore Roosevelt; C. E. Detmold.

Among the distinguished guests invited to meet Professor Goldwin Smith, the following gentlemen were present:

Rev. Dr. Thompson; John A. Stevens; Prof. John W. Draper; Maj.-Gen. B. F. Butler, U. S. A; M. Auguste Laugel, of France; Hon. Geo. Bancroft; Geo. P. Putnam; Dr. Willard Parker; Rev. S. Osgood, D.D.; Hon. E. D. Morgan; Rev. H. Ward Beecher; Rev. A. P. Putnam; Rev. A. Cleveland Coxe, D.D., *Assistant Bishop-elect of the Western Diocese of*

New York; Prof. H. B. Smith, D.D., *Professor of Systematic Theology in Union Theological Seminary, New York;* Chas. King, LL.D. ; Peter Cooper, *Founder of the Cooper Union;* G. W. Curtis; Geo. L. Schuyler; Prof. Theo. W. Dwight, LL.D., *Law Professor in Columbia College;* Rev. G. L. Prentiss, D.D.

Among the letters of regret were notes from Lincoln, Fessenden, Major-General Halleck, and Attorney-General Bates.

www.ingramcontent.com/pod-product-compliance
Lightning Source LLC
Chambersburg PA
CBHW020827230426
43666CB00007B/1134